꿈이 있는

여행 영어

꿈이 있는
여행 영어

김계희 지음

좋은땅

프롤로그

다시금 기지개를 켜고
훌쩍 여행을 떠나고 싶은 시절에

오랫동안 강의한 경험을 바탕으로
「꿈이 있는 여행영어」를 출간하게 되었습니다.

자유여행을 하는 분들은
아는 만큼 소통하고 아는 만큼 느끼면서
자유함을 누리게 되고

패키지여행을 하는 분들도
가이드에게만 의존하지 않고
마주치는 외국인들과 웃으며 소통할 수 있을 겁니다.

필수 표현만 다룬 책이 아니고
대화와 관련된 설명과 추가 표현을 곁들여
이해를 쉽게 하고 응용할 수 있도록 도왔습니다.

꿈꾸는 여행길에 도움이 된다면
더 없는 기쁨으로 여기겠습니다.

2023년 6월에
저자 김계희 드림

차례

Collect moments. Not things.

순간을 모아라. 물건이 아니라

- Karen Salmansohn -

항공권

Dialogue 1. 예약

Clerk : United Airlines. May I help you, ma'am?

Passenger: Yes, please.

I'd like to reserve a ticket to Anchorage.

Clerk : When are you leaving?

Passenger: I'm leaving on July 2nd.

Clerk : What time would you like to make it?

Passenger: I'd like to fly at 3 P.M.

Clerk : Which class would you like?

Passenger: Economy class, please.

Clerk : May I have your name and phone number, please?

Passenger: Yujin Kim. 82-10-0000-0000.

Clerk : Thank you for calling, ma'am.

Passenger: You're welcome.

Notes

▶ ma'am[mǽ(ː)m]: madam[mǽdəm]
여성을 정중히 부르는 존칭. 젊은 여성은 miss가 바람직.

▶ sir: 남성을 정중히 부르는 존칭

▶ reserve a ticket to(for)~: ~행 티켓을 예약하다.
get a ticket to(for)~ : ~행 티켓을 사다.

▶ When are you leaving? = When will you leave?

▸ I'd like to fly at 3 p.m.

I'd like the flight at 3 p.m.

I'd like the 3 p.m. flight. (오후 3시 비행기 원해요)

▸ economy class: 일반석 (economy: ① 경제 ② 절약)

business class: 비지니스석 (= prestige class: 프레스티지석)

first class: 일등석

▸ one way: 편도 ↔ round trip: 왕복

▸ 82-10-0000-0000: 82는 한국 국가번호이고, 국제전화 시
휴대폰 번호 010-0000-0000에서 첫 숫자 0은 생략.

▸ You're welcome.

My pleasure.

Don't mention it.

No problem.

It's nothing.

Of course.

(모두 Thank you!에 대한 인사로 '천만에요'라는 뜻.

이 중 'Of course'는 '당연히 해야 하는 거죠'라는 뉘앙스)

대화 1. 예약

직원: 유나이티드항공입니다. 도와드릴까요?

승객: 네. 앵커리지행 티켓 하나 예약하고 싶은데요.

직원: 언제 떠나십니까?

승객: 7월 2일에 떠날 거예요.

직원: 몇 시로 원하세요?

승객: 오후 3시로 하고 싶습니다.

직원: 어떤 좌석등급을 원하세요?

승객: 일반석 부탁합니다.

직원: 성함과 전화번호가 어떻게 되시죠?

승객: 김유진, 82-10-0000-0000입니다.

직원: 전화 주서서 감사합니다.

승객: 천만에요.

Dialogue 2. 경유 문의

Passenger: Is there a layover?

Clerk   : Yes, you have a layover in Seattle.

Passenger: How long is the layover?

Clerk   : You have to wait for 2 hours there.

Passenger: Is there no direct flight?

Clerk   : Sorry, but there's no non-stop flight.

Notes

▸ layover: 경유지에 머무는 시간이 24시간 미만인 경유.

▸ stopover: 〃   〃   24시간 이상인 경유.

▸ There is + 단수 주어

   There are + 복수 주어 (~가 있다)

   Is there ~

   Are there ~ (~가 있습니까?)

▸ direct flight = non-stop flight (직항)

대화 2. 경유 문의

승객: 경유지가 있나요?

직원: 네, 시애틀에서 경유하십니다.

승객: 경유 시간은 얼마나 되나요?

직원: 거기서 두 시간 기다리셔야 합니다.

승객: 직항은 없나요?

직원: 죄송하지만, 직항은 없습니다.

Dialogue 3. 예약 변경

Passenger: I'd like to change my reservation.

Clerk   : What's your reservation number?

Passenger: It's 3115-0306.

Clerk   : May I have your name?

Passenger: My name is Yujin Kim.

Clerk   : Oh, Ms. Kim. You have a reservation for the 3 p.m. flight on July 2nd, right?

Passenger: Yes, but I'd like to change it to the 2 p.m. flight on July 20th.

Clerk   : Okay.

Notes

▸ I'd like to confirm my reservation. (예약을 확인하고 싶습니다)

     〃   change my reservation. (예약을 변경하고 〃)

     〃   cancel my reservation. (예약을 취소하고 〃)

▸ reservation number = confirmation number (예약/예약확인 번호)

▸ I'd like to = I would like to

▸ I'd like to + V(동사) = I want to + V(동사) (~하기 원하다)

  I'd like   + N(명사) = I want   + N(명사) (~를 원하다)

▸ That flight is booked up.

  That flight is fully booked. (그 비행기는 예약이 다 찼어요.)

대화 3. 예약 변경

승객: 제 예약을 변경하고 싶습니다.

직원: 예약번호가 무엇입니까?

승객: 3115-0306입니다.

직원: 성함이 어떻게 되세요?

승객: 제 이름은 김유진입니다.

직원: 오, Ms. Kim. 7월 2일 오후 3시로 예약이 되어 있네요.
　　맞죠?

승객: 네, 그런데 7월 20일 오후 2시 비행기로 변경하고 싶습니다.

직원: 알겠어요.

※ 달 익히기(1월~12월)

1월 : January	7월 : July
2월 : February	8월 : August
3월 : March	9월 : September
4월 : April	10월 : October
5월 : May	11월 : November
6월 : June	12월 : December

※ 날짜 익히기 (1일~31일)

first	1st	eleventh	11th	twenty first	21st
second	2nd	twelfth	12th	twenty second	22nd
third	3rd	thirteenth	13th	twenty third	23rd
fourth	4th	fourteenth	14th	twenty fourth	24th
fifth	5th	fifteenth	15th	twenty fifth	25th
sixth	6th	sixteenth	16th	twenty sixth	26th
seventh	7th	seventeenth	17th	twenty seventh	27th
eighth	8th	eighteenth	18th	twenty eighth	28th
ninth	9th	nineteenth	19th	twenty ninth	29th
tenth	10th	twentieth	20th	thirtieth	30th
				thirty first	31st

> 날짜는 기수(one, two, three…)가 아닌 서수(first, second, third…)로 위와 같이 사용하세요.

※ 시간 말하기

3:00
It's three o'clock.

3:10
It's three ten.
It's ten past three.

3:15
It's three fifteen.
It's quarter past three.

3:30
It's three thirty.
It's half past three.

3:40
It's three forty.
It's twenty to four.

3:45
It's three forty five.
It's quarter to four.

3:55
It's three fifty five.
It's five to four.

시간 말하는 방법

1. 시간, 분 순서대로 말하기
2. 15분, 45분은 quarter, 30분은 half,
   '전'은 'to', '후'는 'past'를 사용하여 위와 같이 말하기

We travel not to escape life,
but for life not to escape us.

우리는 삶에서 탈출하기 위해 여행하는 것이 아니라
삶이 우리를 달아나지 않게 하기 위해 여행하는 것이다.

- Anonymous -

Clerk : May I see your passport and ticket, please?

Passenger: Here you are.

Clerk : Do you have any seating preference?

Passenger: Aisle seat, please.

If possible, I'd like to get a seat in the first row of economy class seats.

Clerk : Okay. Your seat number is 28D.

Would you put your baggage on the scale?

Passenger: Sure.

Clerk : You must pay for excess weight.

Your baggage is 3kg overweight.

Passenger: How much is it?

Clerk : Sixty dollars.

Passenger: Can I carry this bag with me?

Clerk : Of course. Here's your passport and boarding pass.

Have a nice flight.

Passenger: Thanks a lot.

▶ check in: 공항에서 탑승수속을 밟다. 호텔의 투숙절차를 밟다

▶ passport: 여권. 남성용 지갑을 패스보드라고 부르는 분들이 있는데 이는 잘못된 표현으로 wallet이 맞는 표현.

▶ Sure = Certainly = Of course: 그럼요, 물론요

▶ boarding pass: 탑승권

▶ I'd like to get a seat in the first row of economy class seats.

(일반석 첫 번째 줄에 있는 좌석을 원해요)

I'd like to get a seat next to the emergency exit.

(비상구 옆 좌석을 원해요)

Can I get a seat in the first row of economy class seats?

Can I get a seat next to the emergency exit?

The First Row of Economy Class Seats

'일반석 첫 번째 줄'로 비지니스 좌석 뒤에 있는 그 줄의 좌석은 앞부분에 공간이 넓어 편안합니다. 장애인이나 병약자, 임산부, 만 2세 미만(즉 만 1세까지)의 동반 자녀가 있는 승객의 경우, 추가비용 없이 이용가능하기도 하고, 프리미엄 이코노미라 하여 추가비용을 받기도 합니다. 따라서 항공사나 항공 기종에 따라 상황이 다를 수 있으니 이용하는 항공사의 홈페이지나 고객센터를 통해 자세한 정보를 확인하는 것이 좋습니다.

직원: 여권과 항공권을 보여주시겠어요?

승객: 여기 있습니다.

직원: 선호하시는 좌석 있습니까?

승객: 통로 쪽 부탁합니다.

　　　가능하다면 일반석 첫 번째 줄 좌석에 앉고 싶어요.

직원: 네. 손님 좌석 번호는 28D입니다.

　　　짐을 저울 위에 올려놓아 주시겠어요?

승객: 그러죠.

직원: 초과 무게 지불하셔야 하네요. 3kg 초과되었어요.

승객: 얼마입니까?

직원: 60불입니다.

승객: 이 가방은 갖고 들어가도 되나요?

직원: 물론입니다. 여기 여권과 탑승권이 있습니다.

　　　즐거운 여행 되세요.

승객: 감사합니다.

More Expressions

1. I'd like a window seat. (창가 좌석을 원합니다)
   a middle seat. (가운데 좌석을 원합니다)
   an aisle seat. (통로 쪽 좌석을 원합니다)

▸ aisle: 통로. s는 묵음.

2. What's the flying time from here to Sydney?
   (이곳에서 시드니까지 비행시간이 얼마나 됩니까?)

   It's about 10 hours.
   (약 10 시간입니다)

3. What's the time difference between Seoul and LA?
   (서울에서 LA사이 시차가 얼마나 됩니까?)

   Seoul is 16 hours ahead of L. A.
   (서울은 L. A. 보다 16시간 빠릅니다)

   L. A is 16 hours behind Seoul.
   (L. A. 는 서울보다 16시간 늦습니다)

Life begins
at the end of your comfort zone.

삶은 당신의 안전지대를 벗어나야 비로소 시작된다.

- Neale Donald Walsch -

보안 검색

Dialogue 1. 액체류, 젤류

Screener : Please empty your pockets.

Do you have any liquids or gels in your bag?

Passenger: Yes, I do. I have a water bottle.

Screener : You can either drink it right now or throw it away.

Passenger: I'll just throw it out.

Dialogue 2. 금속류

Screener : Please take off your shoes and belt.

Passenger: Okay.

Screener : Do you have any metal in your pockets?

Passenger: No, I don't.

Screener : Can I search your bag?

Passenger: Sure.

Screener : You can't take this on the plane.

Passenger: I forgot it was in there.

Notes

▸ empty: ① 형용사) 텅 빈

② 동사) 비우다

(자음 3개 mpt의 가운데 p는 탈락되어 '엠티'로 발음)

▸ either A or B: A이거나 B (둘 중 하나 선택)

▸ take off: ① (옷 등을) 벗다, 벗기다 ↔ 입다 put on(동작), wear(상태)

② 이륙하다 (이륙: take-off)

대화 1. 액체류, 젤류

검색직원: 주머니를 비워 주세요.

액체류나 젤류 가방 안에 있습니까?

승객   : 네, 물병이 있어요.

검색직원: 바로 마시거나 버리시면 됩니다.

승객   : 그냥 버릴게요.

대화 2. 금속류

검색직원: 신발과 벨트를 벗어 주세요.

승객   : 네.

검색직원: 주머니에 금속류 있습니까?

승객   : 없어요.

검색직원: 가방을 살펴봐도 될까요?

승객   : 물론요.

검색요원: 이것은 기내로 반입할 수 없습니다.

승객   : 그게 거기 있는 것을 깜박했네요.

More Expressions

1. Please walk through the metal detector.
   (금속 탐지기를 통과해 주십시오)

2. Please walk through again.
   (다시 통과해 주세요)

3. I'm going to scan your body.
   (당신 몸을 스캔하겠습니다)

4. I didn't know this was prohibited.
   (이것이 금지 품목인지 몰랐습니다)

5. All right. You are all clear. Everything looks fine now.
   (좋아요. 이상 없어요. 다 괜찮습니다)

All journeys have secret destinations
of which the traveler is unaware.

모든 여행은
여행자가 알지 못하는 비밀스런 목적지가 있다.

- Martin Buber -

Dialogue 1. 탑승 시

Flight Attendant: May I see your boarding pass?

Passenger   : Here you are.

Flight Attendant: Walk down the aisle.

And your seat will be by the window.

Passenger   : Thank you.

Dialogue 2. 자리 이동 요청

Passenger 1: Excuse me. Can I get by?

Passenger 2: Sure. Go ahead.

·················

Passenger 1: Excuse me.

Would you change your seat with me?

I'd like to sit with my friend.

Passenger 3: No problem.

Notes

▶ Flight Attendant: 승무원

이전엔 성별에 따라 남승무원은 steward, 여승무원은 stewardess로 사용했지만,
요즘에는 성별 중립적인 용어인 flight attendant를 사용하는 것이 일반적.

▸ Here you are. Here it is.
Here you go.

There you are. There it is.
There you go.

모두 '여기 있어요'라는 의미.
Here it goes, There it goes는 사용할 수 없음에 유의하세요.

▸ Can I get by?
Can I go through?
Can you let me through?
(제가 지나가도 될까요?)

* get by: ① 지나가다
② (검열 따위) 통과하다
③ 그럭저럭 살아가다
I just get by. 그냥 지내는 거죠.
I have to get by. 그럭저럭 살아야죠.
* go through: ① 통과하다, 빠져 나가다
② (시련, 어려움을) 겪다, 세파를 겪다
③ ~을 검토하다, 조사하다, 살펴보다

대화 1. 탑승 시

승무원: 탑승권 좀 볼 수 있을까요?

승객　: 여기 있어요.

승무원: 통로로 쭉 내려가세요.

　　　　그러면 손님 좌석은 창가에 있을 거예요.

승객　: 감사해요.

대화 2. 자리 이동 요청

승객 1: 실례합니다. 지나가도 될까요?

승객 2: 물론이죠. 그러세요.

　　　　........................

승객 1: 실례합니다. 좌석을 저랑 바꿔 주시겠어요?

　　　　친구랑 함께 앉고 싶어서요.

승객 3: 그러세요.

Dialogue 3. 이륙 전

Flight Attendant: We will take off shortly.
Please fasten your seat belt and put up your tray table. And return your seat to the upright position.
Passenger : **Okay.**
Flight Attendant: Would you put your bag under your seat? And you are not allowed to use electronics.

Notes

▶ short 짧은, 짧게   shortly 곧
  late 늦은, 늦게   lately 최근에 (recently)
  near 가까운, 가까이   nearly 거의 (almost)
  high 높은, 높게   highly 매우
  hard 열심인, 열심히   hardly 거의 ~하지 않다

▶ Fasten your seat belt(좌석 벨트를 하세요)에서 fasten[fǽsn]의 't' 발음은 묵음.
▶ upright: ① 직립한, 똑바로, 수직의
         ② 곧은, 청렴한, 강직한, 정직한
▶ are allowed to ~   : ~하도록 허락되다
  are not allowed to ~ : ~하도록 허락되지 않다

대화 3. 이륙 전

승무원: 저희는 곧 이륙할 겁니다.

　　　　안전벨트를 착용하시고 접이식 테이블은 올려 주세요.

　　　　그리고 좌석은 똑바로 세워 주세요.

승객　: 알겠어요.

승무원: 가방을 좌석 밑으로 넣어 주시겠어요?

　　　　그리고 전자제품은 사용하실 수 없습니다.

Dialogue 4. 음료

Flight Attendant: Would you like a drink?

Passenger   : Yes, please. What do you have?

Flight Attendant: We have orange juice, tomato juice, Coke, and Seven-up.

Passenger   : Orange juice, please.

Flight Attendant: Here you are.

Passenger   : Thanks. By the way, when is the in-flight meal served?

Flight Attendant: In an hour.

Passenger   : Could you wake me up at meal time?

Flight Attendant: Okay.

Passenger   : Thanks a lot.

Notes

▶ in-flight meal: 기내식

대화 4. 음료

승무원: 음료 드시겠어요?

승객　: 네, 뭐가 있나요?

승무원: 오렌지주스, 토마토주스, 콜라, 사이다가 있습니다.

승객　: 오렌지주스 부탁해요.

승무원: 여기 있어요.

승객　: 고마워요. 그런데 기내식은 언제 나오나요?

승무원: 한 시간 후에요.

승객　: 식사 시간에 저 좀 깨워 주시겠어요?

승무원: 네.

승객　: 고마워요.

Dialogue 5. 기내식

Flight Attendant: Would you like fish or chicken?

Passenger 1 : **Chicken, please.**

Flight Attendant: How about you?

Passenger 2 : **I don't feel like eating now.**

I'd like to skip the meal.

·····························

Passenger 1 : **I'm done. Would you clear the table?**

Flight Attendant: Okay.

Notes

▸ Would you like fish or chicken?

(생선요리 드실래요? 아니면 닭고기 요리 드실래요?)

Fish or chicken?, Beef or chicken? (간단히)

I'd like fish. / I'd like beef. / I'd like chicken.

Fish, please. / Beef, please. / Chicken, please.

▸ How about you? = What about you?

▸ feel like ~ing: ~ 할 것 같다

▸ I'm done. = I'm finished.

대화 5. 기내식

승무원: 생선 요리 드릴래요? 아니면 닭고기 요리 드실래요?

승객 1: 닭고기 요리로 주세요.

승무원: 당신은요?

승객 2: 전 지금 먹고 싶지 않아요. 식사하지 않겠어요.

....

승객 1: 저 다 먹었어요. 테이블 좀 치워 주시겠어요?

승무원: 네.

Dialogue 6. 비행기 멀미

Passenger　　　: Excuse me. I feel very sick.

Flight Attendant: What's wrong with you?

Passenger　　　: I feel like vomiting and I'm dizzy.

　　　　　　　　Do you have pills for air sickness?

Flight Attendant: Yes, we have. I'll get you some medicine.

　　　　　　　　You'll feel better after taking it.

Passenger　　　: Thank you.

　　　　　　　　And I feel chilly. Can I get one more blanket?

Flight Attendant: No problem.

대화 6. 비행기 멀미

승객　: 실례합니다. 제가 몸이 안 좋아요.

승무원: 어디가 안 좋으세요?

승객　: 토할 것 같고 현기증이 나요.

　　　비행기 멀미에 먹는 약 있으세요?

승무원: 네, 있어요. 약을 좀 갖다 드릴게요.

　　　약 드시면 좀 나아질 거예요.

승객　: 고맙습니다.

　　　그리고 제가 한기를 느끼는데요.

　　　담요 한 장만 더 받을 수 있을까요?

승무원: 그럼요.

1. Is the plane <u>on schedule</u>? (비행기가 예정대로 뜹니까?)
   ahead of schedule? (예정보다 일찍)
   behind schedule? (예정보다 늦게)

2. Can I recline my seat? (제 의자 좀 눕혀도 될까요?)

3. May I have something <u>to drink</u>? (마실 것을 들어도 되나요?)
   to read? (읽을 것 좀 있나요?)

4. What would you like to drink? (무엇을 마시고 싶으세요?)
   I'd like <u>Coke</u>, please. (콜라 원합니다)
   Seven-up   (사이다)
   orange juice   (오렌지주스)
   tomato juice   (토마토주스)
   water   (물)
   beer   (맥주)
   whisky   (위스키)
   red/white wine (적/백포도주)

Notes

▶ soda pop, soda, pop: 탄산음료 (일반명사)
▶ Coke, Coca Cola: 콜라의 상표명
▶ Seven-up, Sprite: 사이다의 상표명
▶ 한국의 사이다: 영어로 clear soda
▶ 영어의 cider: 알코올성 사과음료
   - hard cider: 사과즙을 발효시킨 것
   - sweet cider: 사과즙을 발효시키지 않은 것

5. Would you get me a blanket?
   (제게 담요를 한 장 갖다 주시겠습니까?)

6. Do you have a pill for air sickness?
   (비행기 멀미에 먹는 약 있으세요?)

7. A: What's wrong with you? (어디가 안 좋으세요?)
   B: I have a headache. (두통)
   　　　　a toothache. (치통)
   　　　　a cold. (감기)
   　　　　a fever. (열)
   　　　　a sore throat. (목이 아픔)
   　　　　a runny nose. (콧물)
   　　　　a stuffy nose. (코 막힘)
   　　　　a cough. (기침)
   　　　　a stomachache. (위통)
   　　　　an upset stomach. (위통)
   　　　　a backache. (요통)
   　　　　a hangover. (숙취)
   　　　　a tightness in my chest. (가슴이 답답)
   　　　　ringing in my ears. (이명)
   　　　　jet lag. (시차로 인한 피로감, 시차증)

   I have <u>motion</u> sickness. I am <u>motion</u> sick. (멀미를 해요)
   　　　car　　　　　　　car　　　　(차멀미)
   　　　sea　　　　　　　sea　　　　(뱃멀미)
   　　　air　　　　　　　air　　　　(비행기 멀미)

I have diarrhea. [daiəríə] = I have the runs. (설사해요)

I have indigestion. (소화불량이에요)

I have no appetite. (식욕이 없어요)

My tonsils are swollen. (편도가 부었어요)

I've been sneezing. (재채기를 계속해요)

I feel dizzy. (현기증이 나요)

I feel nauseous. (구역질을 해요)

I'm constipated. (변비가 있어요)

I twisted my ankle. (발목을 삐었어요)

I broke my arm. (팔이 부러졌어요)

I burned my hand. (손을 데었어요)

I cut my finger. (손가락을 베었어요)

I ache all over. (온몸이 쑤셔요)

I am homesick. (집 생각이 나요)

※ 이명, 시차증, 멀미, 설사, 소화불량 등의 단어 앞엔 관사 'a, an, the'를 사용하지 않습니다.

《Announcements (안내 방송)》

1. Paging Announcements (사람을 찾는 안내 방송)

Paging Mr. Kennedy. Please contact the American Airlines ticket counter immediately.
케네디 씨를 찾습니다. 아메리카항공 티켓 카운터로 즉시 연락바랍니다.

Notes

▶ page: 동사) 호텔, 공항 등에서 사람을 찾다

2. Announcements in the Lobby (로비 안내 방송)

American Airlines announces the departure of Flight 800 bound for New York via Fairbanks. Passengers on this flight should proceed to Gate 23.
아메리카항공에서 훼어뱅크스를 경유하여 뉴욕으로 가는 800편의 출발을 알려드립니다. 이편을 이용하실 승객 여러분은 23번 게이트로 가시기 바랍니다.

Notes

▶ bound for~: ~행의
▶ via: ~을 경유하여, ~을 통하여
▶ proceed to: ~로 나아가다

United Airlines Flight 906 bound for Hongkong is now boarding.
Passengers on this flight should board.
홍콩행 유나이티드항공 906편이 탑승 중에 있습니다. 이편을 이용하실
승객 여러분은 탑승해 주시기 바랍니다.

Attention, please! This is the last call for Lufthansa Flight 653 bound
for Frankfurt. All passengers departing on this flight should be on
board.
여러분께 알려 드립니다. 프랑크푸르트행 루프트한자 653편의 마지막
탑승안내를 드립니다. 이 항공편으로 출발하시는 승객 여러분은 탑승
해 주시기 바랍니다.

Notes
▶ last call: 마지막 탑승안내

3. Flight Delay (항공기 지연)

The departure of Korean Air Lines Flight 72 for Honolulu is being
delayed because of bad weather.
호놀룰루행 대한항공 72편의 출발이 기후 불순으로 지연되고 있습니다.

Notes
▶ is being delayed: 지연되고 있다
　현재 진행형의 수동태 (be + being + p.p.)
▶ because of: 전치사) ~ 때문에
　(= due to, owing to, on account of)

4. Flight Cancellation (항공기 결항)

Ladies and gentlemen. We are afraid we must cancel the flight because of mechanical difficulties. We apologize for the inconvenience. The new departure time will be around eight o'clock tomorrow morning, so we have arranged for your transportation and accommodations for tonight. We ask for your kind understanding and cooperation in this unexpected situation.

신사 숙녀 여러분. 죄송합니다만 기계사정으로 결항하지 않으면 안 되었습니다. 불편을 드려 사과 말씀드립니다. 다음 출발시간은 내일 아침 8시경이 되겠습니다. 그래서 오늘밤 교통편과 숙박을 마련해 놓았습니다. 이 뜻밖의 상황에 여러분의 친절한 이해와 협조를 부탁드립니다.

5. Announcements on the Plane (기내 안내 방송)

Good afternoon, ladies and gentlemen. We welcome you aboard our Boeing 747 flight bound for New York. This is your captain speaking. We are now cruising at an altitude of 33,000 feet, which is 10,000 meters, sky high. And an air speed of 550 miles or 880 kilometers per hour. We are now flying in a very good condition.

신사 숙녀 여러분, 안녕하세요. 뉴욕행 보잉 747 탑승을 환영합니다. 저는 기장입니다. 우리는 현재 고도 33,000 피트 즉 10,000 미터, 시속 550 마일 즉 880 km로 순조롭게 비행 중입니다.

Notes

▶ cruise: 비행하다, 순항하다
▶ at an altitude of~: 고도 ~로
▶ sky high: 매우 높게, 까마득히 높게

We have departed Seoul 20 minutes behind schedule, but we now have strong tail winds, so we estimate our arrival in New York John F. Kennedy International Airport on schedule.

저희는 서울에서 예정보다 20분 늦게 출발하였지만, 현재 강한 순풍을 타고 뉴욕 존 F 케네디 국제공항에는 예정대로 도착하리라 생각합니다.

Notes

▶ behind schedule: 예정보다 늦게
  ahead of schedule: 예정보다 이르게
  on schedule: 예정대로
▶ tail wind: (항공, 항선) 뒤에서 부는 바람, 뒷바람, 순풍

A satellite shows New York area weather should be fair and temperature on the ground is 77 degrees F or 24 degrees C. The weather enroute should be generally good, but we may have a few choppy areas. So I do recommend you keep your seat belt fastened while you are seated, against unexpected turbulence.

위성 이미지에 따르면, 뉴욕 지역의 날씨는 맑고, 지상 온도는 화씨 77도, 즉 섭씨 24도입니다. 항로상의 기후는 대체로 양호한 편이지만, 기후가 나쁜 곳을 몇 차례 통과할 가능성이 있으므로 갑작스런 흔들림에 대비하여 앉아 계시는 동안 좌석벨트를 하고 계시기 바랍니다.

Notes

▶ 77 degrees F: 화씨 77도 (F: Fahrenheit → 화씨)
▶ 24 degrees C: 섭씨 24도 (C: Centigrade 또는 Celsius → 섭씨)
▶ enroute: 항로상의
▶ turbulence: 흔들림, (대기의) 난류

We are now flying over the city of Anchorage, Alaska and we will be in New York in about 7 hours. Enjoy and relax during the entire flight. Thank you so much.

현재 비행기는 알래스카주 앵커리지 상공을 통과하고 있고, 약 7시간 후에 저희는 뉴욕에 도착하게 됩니다. 즐겁고 편안한 여행되시길 바랍니다. 대단히 감사합니다.

Ladies and gentlemen. We shall be arriving in LA shortly, at four o'clock local time.

신사 숙녀 여러분. 곧 현지 시각 4시에 저희는 LA에 도착하게 됩니다.

Notes

▶ at four o'clock local time: 현지 시각 4시에

We are now approaching Los Angeles International Airport. Please fasten your seat belt and put seatback and table in the upright position.

저희는 지금 LA 국제공항에 접근하고 있습니다. 좌석벨트를 매어 주시고 좌석 등받이와 테이블을 원 위치해 주시기 바랍니다.

Notes

▶ put A in the upright position: A를 원위치로 세우다
▶ upright: 직립한, 똑바로, 수직의, 곧은, 청렴한, 강직한, 정직한

Passengers, please remain seated until the aircraft has come to a complete halt.

승객 여러분, 항공기가 완전히 멈출 때까지 좌석에 앉아 계시기 바랍니다.

We hope you have had a pleasant flight, and that you'll fly with us again. Thank you.
즐거운 여행이 되셨길 바라며, 앞으로 다시 모실 수 있기를 바랍니다. 감사합니다.

The journey not the arrival matters.

중요한 것은 도착이 아니라 여정이다.

- T. S. Eliot -

Dialogue 1. 환승 문의

Traveler: Excuse me! I'm a transfer passenger for Anchorage.
Where is the transfer counter?

Man   : You should go that way.

....

Traveler: I have to take a connecting flight.
Which gate should I go to?

Staff   : What's your final destination?

Traveler: It's Anchorage.

Staff   : Go to Gate 36.

Traveler: Thanks. Do I have to claim my baggage here and
recheck it?

Staff   : No, you need not.

Notes

▶ connecting flight: 연결 항공편
▶ final destination: 최종 목적지
▶ claim baggage: 수하물을 찾다
▶ check baggage: 수하물을 부치다
　 recheck baggage:　　〃　　다시 부치다

대화 1. 환승 문의

**여행자: 실례합니다! 저는 앵커리지 가는 환승객인데요.
환승 수속대가 어디에 있나요?**

남자 : 저쪽으로 가서야 해요.

....

**여행자: 제가 연결 항공편을 타야 하는데요.
몇 번 탑승구로 가야 하나요?**

직원 : 최종 목적지가 어디인가요?

여행자: 앵커리지입니다.

직원 : 36번 탑승구로 가세요.

여행자: 감사합니다. 제가 수하물을 여기서 찾아 다시 부쳐야 하나요?

직원 : 아니요. 그러실 필요 없습니다.

Dialogue 2. 연결 항공편을 놓쳤을 때

Traveler: My flight was delayed in Seoul and
I missed my connecting flight.

Staff　　: What's your flight number?

Traveler: It's KE 203.
When is the next flight to Anchorage?

Staff　　: Let me check if we have another flight.
The next available flight is at 6:30 p. m.
We'll get you on that flight.

Traveler: Thanks.

Notes

▸ miss　　: 동사) 그리워하다, (기차/버스 등을) 놓치다
missing: 형용사) 실종된, 행방불명의

▸ Let me check if ~
I will check if ~ (~인지 제가 확인할게요)

대화 2. 연결 항공편을 놓쳤을 때

여행자: 서울에서 비행기가 연착되어서 제가 연결 항공편을 놓쳤어요.

직원　: 항공편명이 무엇이죠?

여행자: KE 203입니다.

앵커리지 가는 다음 비행기는 언제 있나요?

직원　: 다른 항공편이 있는지 알아봐 드릴게요.

다음 이용 가능한 비행기는 오후 6시 30분에 있네요.

그 비행기에 탑승시켜 드리겠습니다.

여행자: 감사합니다.

More Expressions

1. I'm a transfer passenger. Which terminal should I go to?
   (저는 환승객입니다. 어느 터미널로 가야하나요?)

2. Can I take an alternative flight as soon as possible?
   (가능한 빨리 제가 대체 항공편을 탈 수 있나요?)

3. Can you help me find an alternative flight?
   (제가 대체 항공편 찾는 것 좀 도와주시겠어요?)

4. Should I claim my baggage here and recheck it?
   (제 수하물을 여기서 찾아서 다시 부쳐야 하나요?)

5. Can I get out of the airport during a layover?
   (경유지에 있는 동안 공항을 나갈 수 있나요?)

6. Do you have any staff who can speak Korean?
   (한국어 하는 직원분이 있나요?)

※ Transfer vs. Transit

· **Transfer**: 최종 목적지로 가기 전에 타고 있던 비행기를 **'다른 비행기'** 로 갈아타는 환승

· **Transit**: 목적지로 가기 전에 추가 탑승이나 급유, 급수, 기내식 보충 등을 위해 비행기에서 내려 대기하다 **'같은 비행기'**를 타는 환승. 이때 기내에서 대기할 수도 있고 공항 대합실에서 대기할 경우도 있는데, 후자의 경우 귀중품이 든 수화물은 지참하는 것이 안전함.

Traveling is a return to the essentials.

여행은 본질로의 회귀다.

- Tibetan proverb -

Immigration Officer: May I see your passport and arrival card?

Traveler : **Here you are.**

Immigration Officer: What's the purpose of your visit?

Traveler : **I'm here on vacation.**

Immigration Officer: What's your occupation?

Traveler : **I'm a public official.**

Immigration Officer: How long will you stay?

Traveler : **I will stay for 10 days.**

Immigration Officer: Where are you going to stay?

Traveler : **At the Grand Hotel.**

Immigration Officer: Okay. Have a nice trip!

Traveler : **Thank you.**

입국심사직원: 여권과 입국 카드를 볼 수 있을까요?

여행자 : **여기 있어요.**

입국심사직원: 방문 목적이 무엇입니까?

여행자 : **휴가차 왔습니다.**

입국심사직원: 직업이 무엇입니까?

여행자 : **전 공무원이에요.**

입국심사직원: 얼마 동안 체류하십니까?

여행자 : **10일 동안 있을 겁니다.**

입국심사직원: 어디서 체류하십니까?

여행자 : **그랜드 호텔이요.**

입국심사직원: 즐거운 여행 되세요.

여행자 : **감사합니다.**

1. What's the purpose of your visit?
   (방문 목적이 무엇입니까?)
   May I ask what brings you here?
   May I ask what brought you here?
   (방문 목적이 뭔지 여쭤 봐도 될까요?)

   I'm here for sightseeing. (관광차)
   I'm here on holiday. (휴가차)
   I'm here on vacation. (휴가차)
   I'm here on business. (업무차/출장차)
   I'm here on an overseas study tour. (해외연수차)
   I'm here on honeymoon. (신혼여행)
   I'm here to study. (공부)
   I'm here to visit my friend. (친구 방문)
   I'm here to visit my son/daughter. (아들/딸 방문)
   I'm here to visit my relatives. (친지 방문)

2. What's your job?
   What's your occupation?
   What do you do (for a living)?
   What business are you in?
   What line of work are you in?
   (직업이 무엇입니까?)

I'm a public official. (저는 공무원입니다)

  a public officer.

  a public employee.

  a public servant.

  a government official.

  a government officer.

  a government employee.

  a civil servant.

I'm a student. (학생)

I'm a teacher. (교사)

I'm a housewife. (주부)

I'm a salesman/saleswoman. (영업사원)

I'm a salaried worker. (회사원)

I'm in between jobs. (취업 준비 중)

I'm retired. (은퇴했어요)

Additional Vocabulary (추가 어휘)

writer(작가), painter(화가), musician(음악가), singer(가수), movie star(배우), athlete(운동선수), personal trainer(PT 트레이너), swimming instructor(수영 강사), police officer(경찰), farmer(농부), fisherman/fisherwoman(어부), realtor(공인중개사), taxi/bus driver(택시/버스 운전기사), pastor(목사), priest(신부), nun(수녀), Buddhist nun(여승), monk(스님), doctor(의사), Korean medicine doctor(한의사), dentist(치과의사), nurse(간호사), business man/business woman(사업가), professor(교수), photographer(사진작가), tax accountant(세무사), certified public accountant/chartered accountant(공인회계사), researcher(연구원), lawyer(변호사)

3. Where do you work? (어디서 근무하세요?)

    I work at the Chungnam Provincial Office. (충남도청)
              the Asan City Hall. (아산시청)
              the Buyeo County Office. (부여군청)
              the Yeonmu Town Office. (연무읍사무소)
              the Duma Township Office. (두마면사무소)
    I work for the ABC Company. (ABC 회사)

4. How long will you stay? (미래)
    How long are you staying? (현재 진행 → 가까운 미래)
    How long are you going to stay? (be going to+동사원형)
    How long will you be staying? (미래 진행)
    (얼마 동안 체류하십니까?)

    I will stay for 10 days.
    I am staying for 10 days.
    I am going to stay for 10 days.
    I will be staying for 10 days.
    (10일 동안 체류합니다)

The journey itself is my home.

여행은 그 자체로 내 집이다.

- Matsuo Basho -

수하물 찾기/분실

Traveler: Excuse me, where is the baggage claim area?
            I can't locate the carousel for UA735.

            ....

Traveler: I think I lost my baggage. It is missing.
            Can you help me to find my baggage?
Staff   : Can I see your baggage claim tag?
Traveler: Here it is. Please send it to my hotel if you find it.

Notes

▸ locate: 정확한 위치를 찾아내다

▸ carousel: (공항의 회전식 원형) 수하물 컨베이어 벨트

▸ missing: 형용사) 실종된, 행방불명의

  miss   : 동사) 그리워하다, 기차/버스 등을) 놓치다

▸ help 목적어 V (동사원형)

  help 목적어 to V (to 부정사): 목적어가 ~하는 것을 돕다

  - 'help'는 준사역동사로 목적어 다음에 '동사원형'이 올 수도 있고 'to 부정사'가
    올 수도 있습니다.

여행자: 실례지만, 수하물 찾는 곳이 어디죠?
　　　　UA735편 수하물 컨베이어를 못 찾겠어요.
···

여행자: 제 짐을 잃어버린 것 같아요. 없어졌어요.
　　　　제 짐 찾는 것 좀 도와주시겠어요?
직원　：수하물표를 좀 볼 수 있을까요?
여행자: 여기 있어요. 찾으시면 제 호텔로 보내 주세요.

Wherever you go,
go with all your heart.

어디를 가든 마음을 다해 가라.

- Confucius -

Customs Officer: Do you have anything to declare?

Traveler   **: No, nothing.**

I just bought a carton of cigarettes and

a bottle of wine.

Customs Officer: Could you open your bag?

Traveler   **: Sure. I just have my personal belongings.**

Customs Officer: What's this for?

Traveler   **: It's a gift for my friend.**

Customs Officer: You have to pay duty on this.

Traveler   **: How much do I have to pay?**

Notes

▶ personal belongings = personal effects (개인 소지품)

▶ pay duty on ~: ~에 대해 관세를 지불하다

세관직원: 신고할 물품이 있으신가요?

여행자   : 아니요, 없습니다.

저는 담배 한 보루와 와인 한 병만 샀는데요.

세관직원: 가방 좀 열어 봐 주시겠어요?

여행자   : 그러죠. 단지 개인 소지품만 있습니다.

세관직원: 이건 뭐죠?

여행자   : 제 친구 줄 선물이에요.

세관직원: 관세를 지불하셔야 합니다.

여행자   : 얼마를 내야 하나요?

1. Do you have anything to declare?
   (신고할 물품이 있으십니까?)

   A. No, nothing.
      No, I have <u>nothing</u> to declare. (아니오, 없습니다)

   B. Yes, I have <u>something</u> to declare.
      (네, 신고할 것 있습니다)

      Yes, I have <u>a bottle of liquor</u> to declare. (술 한 병)
      <u>a carton of cigarettes</u> to declare. (담배 한 보루)
      <u>a camera</u> to declare. (카메라)

2. May I close my bag? (제 가방을 닫아도 되겠습니까?)

3. <u>Should I</u> pay duty on this?
   <u>Do I have to</u> pay duty on this?
   (이 물건에 대해 관세를 지불해야만 합니까?)

   * **should = have to** (~ 해야만 하다)
     I should ~ = I have to ~ (전 ~해야만 합니다)
     Should I ~ = Do I have to ~ (제가 ~해야만 합니까?)

   의문문으로 사용할 때, 조동사 should는 주어 앞으로 나와 'Should I ~'
   라 하지만 have to는 do동사를 사용하여 'Do I have to~'로 표현합니다.

※ 입국 신고서

Please complete clearly in English and BLOCK CAPITALS.
영문 대문자로 정확히 작성해 주세요.

Family name 성	HONG	
First name 이름	KILDONG	

Sex 성별

☑ M   ☐ F

Date of birth 생년월일

D	D	M	M	Y	Y	Y	Y
2	0	0	3	2	0	1	1

Town and Country of birth 출생 국가 도시

DAEJEON

Nationality 국적

KOREA

Occupation 직업

BUSINESSMAN

Contact address in the UK(in full) 영국 내 상세 주소

CLASSIC HOTEL, 92 SUSSEX GARDENS,

LONDON W2 1UH, UNITED KINGDOM

Passport no. 여권 번호

M12345678

Place of issue 여권 발급지

DAEJEON

Length of stay in the UK 영국 내 체류기간
5 DAYS

Port of last departure 최종 출발지
INCHEON

Arrival flight / Train number / Ship name 입국 비행기 편명/기차 편명/선박 편명
KE 907

Signature 서명

IF YOU BREAK UK LAWS, YOU COULD FACE IMPRISONMENT AND REMOVAL.
만일 영국법을 어길 경우, 구속되거나 추방될 수 있습니다.

CAT	-16	CODE	NAT	POL

※ 입국 신고서 작성요령

1. Family name/Last name/Surname: 성
2. First name/Given name: 이름
3. Sex: 성별 M: 남성 F: 여성
4. Date of Birth DD/MM/YYYY: 생년월일 일/월/년
5. Town and Country of Birth: 출생국가 도시
6. Nationality: 국적
7. Occupation: 직업
8. Contact Address in the UK (in full): 영국 내 상세주소
9. Passport No.: 여권 번호
10. Place of Issue: 여권 발급장소
11. Length of Stay in the UK: 영국 내 체류기간
12. Port of Last Departure: 최종 출발지
13. Arrival Flight/Train Number/Ship Name:
    입국 비행기 편명/기차 편명/선박 편명
14. Signature: 서명

Notes

▶ 입국 신고서:
  Arrival Card, Landing Card, Incoming Card, Disembarkation Card

▶ 각국의 입국 신고서는 용어가 비슷하므로 여행 전에 한 국가의 작성 요령을 익혀
  놓으면 좋습니다. 전자여행허가서(미국: ESTA, 한국: K-ETA)로 여행허가를 받은
  여행자는 입국신고서를 별도로 작성할 필요는 없습니다.

※ 세관 신고서

WELCOME TO THE UNITED STATES

DEPARTMENT OF THE TREASURY
UNITED STATES CUSTOMS SERVICE
FORM APPROVED
OMB NO. 1515-0041

CUSTOMS DECLARATION

19 CFR 122.27, 148.12, 148.13, 148.110, 148.111

Each arriving traveler or head of family must provide the following information (only **ONE** written declaration per family is required):

1. Name: _____ _____ _____
   Last   First   Middle Initial

2. Date of Birth: ____|____|____ 3. Airline/Flight _____
   Day Month Year

4. Number of family members traveling with you _____

5. U.S. Address: _____

   City: _____ State: _____

6. I am a U.S. Citizen   YES   NO
   If No,   ☐   ☐
   Country: _____

7. I reside permanently in the U.S.   YES   NO
   If No,   ☐   ☐
   Expected Length of Stay: _____

8. The purpose of my trip is or was ☐ BUSINESS   ☐ PLEASURE

9. I am/we are bringing fruits, plants, meats, food,   YES   NO
   soil, birds, snails, other live animals, farm   ☐   ☐
   products, or I/we have been on a farm or ranch
   outside the U.S.

10. I am/we are carrying currency or monetary   YES   NO
    instruments over $10,000 U.S. or foreign   ☐   ☐
    equivalent.

11. The total value of all goods I/we purchased or
    acquired abroad and am/are bringing to the U.S.
    is (see instructions under Merchandise on reverse
    side): $ _____
                                                US Dollars

▶ **MOST MAJOR CREDIT CARDS ACCEPTED.**

SIGN ON REVERSE SIDE AFTER YOU READ WARNING.
(Do not write below this line.)

INSPECTOR'S NAME   STAMP AREA

BADGE NO.

Paperwork Reduction Act Notice: The Paperwork Reduction Act of 1980 says we must tell you why we are collecting this information, how we will use it and whether you have to give it to us. We ask for this information to carry out the Customs, Agriculture, and Currency laws of the United States. We need it to ensure that travelers are complying with these laws and to allow us to figure and collect the right amount of duties and taxes. Your response is mandatory.

Statement required by 5 CFR 1320.21: The estimated average burden associated with this collection of information is 3 minutes per respondent or recordkeeper depending on individual circumstances. Comments concerning the accuracy of this burden estimate and suggestions for reducing this burden should be directed to U.S. Customs Service, Paperwork Management Branch, Washington, DC 20229, and to the Office of Management and Budget, Paperwork Reduction Project (1515-0041), Washington, DC 20503.

Customs Form 6059B (092089)

Notes

▶ 세관 신고서: Customs Declaration

※ 세관 신고서 작성요령

1. **Name**: 성명, **Last**: 성, **First**: 이름, **Middle Initial**: 중간 이름 첫 자

2. **Date of Birth**: **Day/Mo/Yr** 생년월일: 일/월/년

3. **Airline/Flight**: 항공사/항공편명

4. **Number of family members traveling with you**:
   여행 동반 가족 수

5. **U. S. Address**: 미국 주소
   City 도시, **State** 주

6. **I am a U. S. Citizen** 나는 미국 시민입니다

YES	NO
□	□

   If No, 만일 아니면,
   Country 국가명 _____

7. **I reside permanently in the U. S.**
   미국 영주권자입니다

YES	NO
□	□

   If No, 만일 아니면,
   Expected Length of Stay 예상 체류기간

   _____

8. **The purpose of my trip is or was** □ BUSINESS □ PLEASURE
   여행 목적은   업무차   휴가차

9. **I am/we are bringing fruits, plants, meats, food, soil, birds, snails, other live animals, farm products, or I/we have been on a farm or ranch outside the U. S.**

YES	NO
□	□

   나는/우리는 과일, 식물, 고기, 식품, 흙, 새, 달팽이, 다른 살아 있는

동물, 농장제품 등을 반입 중이며, 또는 미국 이외 지역의 농장이나
목장에 다녀온 적이 있습니다.

10. I am/we are carrying currency or monetary instruments over
    $10,000 U. S. or foreign equivalent.

                                          YES   NO
                                           □   □

   나는/우리는 미화 10,000불, 또는 이에 준하는 외화를 소지하고 있
   습니다.

11. The total value of all goods I/we purchased or acquired abroad
    and am/are bringing to the U. S. is US$ _____.

   내가/우리가 구입했거나 해외에서 취득하여 미국에 반입하는 제품
   의 총가는 US Dollars(미화) _____ 입니다.

The fool wanders, a wise man travels.

바보는 방황하고 현자는 여행한다.

- Thomas Fuller -

Traveler: **I'd like to exchange Korean won**
for U.S. dollars.

Staff : How much would you like to change?

Traveler: **500,000 won.**

Staff : How would you like your money?

Traveler: **I'd like it in tens and twenties.**
And some small change, please.

Staff : Okay.

Traveler: **What's the exchange rate?**

Staff : 1,318 won to the U.S. dollar.

Traveler: **What's the exchange fee?**

Staff : 1.75%.

Notes

▸ To U.S. dollars, please.
To euros, please.

I'd like to change this into U.S. dollars.
I'd like to change this into euros.

▸ exchange A for B = change A into B
(A를 B로 환전하다)

▸ exchange rate: 환율, exchange fee: 환전 수수료

▸ bill: 지폐
1 dollar bill, 5 dollar bill, 10 dollar bill, 20 dollar bill,
100 dollar bill (1달러/5달러/10달러/20달러/100달러 지폐)

▸ coin: 동전
(penny: 1센트, nickel: 5센트, dime: 10센트, quarter: 25센트)

여행자: 한화를 미화로 환전하고 싶습니다.

직원   : 얼마 환전해 드릴까요?

여행자: 500,000원요.

직원   : 어떻게 드릴까요?

여행자: 10달러, 20달러짜리로 주세요.
　　　　 잔돈도 좀 주세요.

직원   : 네.

여행자: 환율은 어떻게 됩니까?

직원   : 1달러에 1,318원입니다.

여행자: 환전 수수료는 얼마예요?

직원   : 1.75%예요.

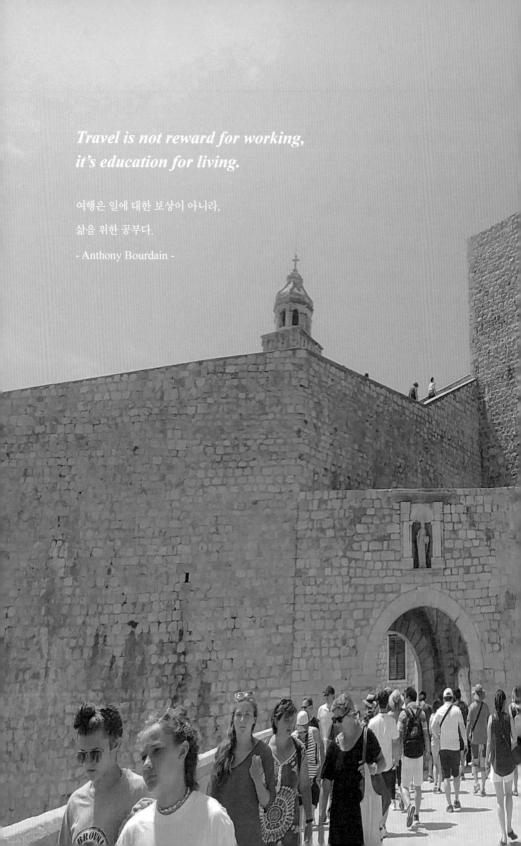

Travel is not reward for working,
it's education for living.

여행은 일에 대한 보상이 아니라,
삶을 위한 공부다.

- Anthony Bourdain -

숙소 예약/체크인/체크아웃

Dialogue 1. 예약 다 찬 경우

Hotel Clerk: Good afternoon! May I help you?

Traveler   : Yes, please.

I'd like to book a double room for May 10th.

Hotel Clerk: Sorry. We are fully booked for now.

There's no vacancy for that day.

Notes

▶ book = reserve: 예약하다

▶ for May 10th: 5월 10일로

(이때 전치사 on이 아닌 **'for'**를 사용함에 유의!)

▶ We are fully booked for now.

We are booked up for now. (지금으로선 예약이 다 찼는데요)

▶ for now: 지금으로서는

▶ vacancy: ① 빈방 ② 공석 (= opening, job opening)

no vacancy: 빈방 없음

(숙박시설 앞쪽에 No Vacancy라는 사인을 세워 놓아 손님이 건물 안으로 들어
오지 않도록 배려하는 곳도 있음)

대화 1. 예약 다 찬 경우

호텔 직원: 안녕하세요? 도와 드릴까요?
여행자　：5월 10일로 더블 룸 하나 예약하고 싶습니다.
호텔 직원: 죄송합니다. 지금으로선 예약이 다 찼습니다.
　　　　　그날엔 빈방이 없네요.

Dialogue 2. 예약

Hotel Clerk: Grand Hotel. May I help you?

Traveler　: I'd like to reserve a room.

Hotel Clerk: What kind of room would you like?

Traveler　: I'd like a single room.

Hotel Clerk: How long will you stay?

Traveler　: I'll stay for 5 days from March 9th to March 13th.

Hotel Clerk: We have a room with a good view of the ocean.

Traveler　: What's the room rate?

Hotel Clerk: 150 dollars a night. Breakfast is included.
　　　　　　The tax and service charges will be added to this rate.

Traveler　: OK. I'll take it.

Notes

▶ room rate : 객실요금 (= room price, room charge)

▶ single room: 1인용 침대가 1개 놓여있는 1인실 방

　 double room: 2인용 침대가 1개 놓여있는 2인실 방

　 twin room: 1인용 침대가 2개 놓여있는 2인실 방

　 suite[swiːt]: 호텔에서 침실 외에 거실, 응접실 등이 붙어 있는 방

　　　　　　 suite 뒤에는 room을 붙이지 않는 것에 유의.

　 dormitory: 공동 침실 (여러 개의 침대가 있는 큰 방)

대화 2. 예약

호텔 직원: Grand Hotel입니다. 도와 드릴까요?

여행자   : 방을 하나 예약하고 싶습니다.

호텔 직원: 어떤 종류의 방을 원하십니까?

여행자   : 싱글 룸 하나 원해요.

호텔 직원: 얼마 동안 체류하십니까?

여행자   : 3월 9일부터 3월 13일까지 5일 동안 체류할 거예요.

호텔 직원: 바다 전망이 좋은 방이 있습니다.

여행자   : 객실 요금은 얼마입니까?

호텔 직원: 하룻밤에 150불입니다. 아침 식사 포함되고요.
　　　　　　세금과 봉사료가 이 요금에 추가될 겁니다.

여행자   : 네, 그 방으로 하죠.

Dialogue 3. 예약 변경/확인/취소

Traveler : **I'd like to change my reservation.**

Hotel Clerk: What name is it under?

Traveler : **Heera Yoon.**

Hotel Clerk: How do you spell it?

Traveler : **H-e-e-r-a Y-o-o-n**

I'd like to change the date to May 15th.

And I'd like a twin room instead of a single.

Notes

▶ I'd like to change my reservation. (제 예약을 변경하고 싶습니다)

    "   confirm   "   ("   확인하고   "   )

    "   cancel   "   ("   취소하고   "   )

▶ first name = given name (이름)

  last name = family name = surname (성)

  full name = first name + last name (이름 + 성)

▶ instead of: ~대신에

대화 3. 예약 변경/확인/취소

여행자 : 제 예약을 변경하고 싶습니다.

호텔 직원: 무슨 성함으로 예약 하셨나요?

여행자 : 윤희라요.

호텔 직원: 성함 철자가 어떻게 되나요?

여행자 : H-e-e-r-a Y-o-o-n

날짜를 5월 15일로 변경하고 싶어요.

그리고 싱글 룸 대신 트윈 룸으로 원해요.

※ 해외여행 시 유용한 앱

- 구글맵(Google map): 세계 지도 어플
- 트립어드바이저(tripadvisor): 실제 여행자 리뷰를 토대로 호텔, 음식 점, 관광명소를 찾을 수 있는 어플
- 에어비앤비(www.airbnb.co.kr): 세계 각국의 현지인들이 살고 있는 가정집을 전 세계 여행자들에게 공유하는 서비스

Dialogue 4. 숙소 체크인

Traveler : Hello! I'd like to check in.

Hotel Clerk: Do you have a reservation?

Traveler : Yes. I made a reservation under Heera Yoon.

Hotel Clerk: Fill out this form, please. Here's your room key,
and this is a voucher for your free breakfast.

Traveler : Thanks. I'd like to check my valuables in your safe.

Hotel Clerk: Okay.

Traveler : What time is check-out?

Notes

▶ check in ↔ check out

▶ Do you have a reservation? (예약한 거 있으세요?)
Did you make a reservation? (예약하셨습니까?)

▶ valuables: 귀중품
I'd like to <u>check</u> my valuables. (제 귀중품을 맡기고 싶습니다)
=   〃   <u>leave</u>   〃   .

I'd like to <u>get</u> my valuables. (제 귀중품을 찾고 싶어요)
=   〃   <u>take out</u>   〃   .

▶ safe: 명사) 금고, 형용사) 안전한

대화 4. 숙소 체크인

여행자 : **안녕하세요? 체크인 하고 싶어요.**

호텔 직원: 예약하신 거 있나요?

여행자 : **네. 윤희라라는 이름으로 예약했어요.**

호텔 직원: 이 양식을 작성해 주세요. 여기 방 키 있습니다.

그리고 이것은 무료 아침식사 쿠폰입니다.

여행자 : **고마워요. 제 귀중품을 호텔 금고에 맡기고 싶은데요.**

호텔 직원: 네.

여행자 : **체크아웃은 몇 시죠?**

Dialogue 5. 편의 시설 (호텔 식당/스파/헬스장/수영장)

Traveler　　: **Where is the restaurant?**
Hotel Clerk: It's on the first floor.
Traveler　　: **What time is breakfast?**
Hotel Clerk: It's from 7 to 10.
Traveler　　: **Is there a spa here?**
Hotel Clerk: Of course.
Traveler　　: **How late is the spa open?**
Hotel Clerk: It's open until 11 p.m.

Notes

▶ 미국) first floor 1층, second floor 2층, third floor 3층,
　　　 fourth floor 4층, fifth floor 5층, sixth floor 6층

　 영국) ground floor 1층, first floor 2층, second floor 3층,
　　　 third floor 4층, fourth floor 5층, fifth floor 6층

▶ Is there a spa here? (여기에 스파 있나요?)
　　 〃　 a fitness center here? (여기 헬스장 있나요?)
　　 〃　 a swimming pool here? (여기 수영장 있나요?)

　 Do you have a spa here? (여기에 스파 있나요?)
　　 〃　　 a fitness center here? (여기 헬스장 있나요?)
　　 〃　　 a swimming pool here? (여기 수영장 있나요?)

▶ How late is the spa open? (얼마나 늦게까지 스파 여나요?)
　　 〃　　 the fitness center open? (〃 　헬스장 여나요?)
　　 〃　　 the swimming pool open? (〃 　수영장 여나요?)

대화 5. 편의 시설 (호텔 식당/스파/헬스장/수영장)

여행자　: 식당이 어디 있나요?

호텔 직원: 1층에 있어요.

여행자　: 아침 식사 시간은요?

호텔 직원: 7시부터 10시까지입니다.

여행자　: 이곳에 스파 있나요?

호텔 직원: 물론요.

여행자　: 얼마나 늦게까지 여나요?

호텔 직원: 오후 11시까지 오픈합니다.

Dialogue 6. 서비스 요청/문의

Traveler   : Hello. This is room 203.

                  Can I have an extra blanket?

Hotel Clerk: Sure. I will bring it right away.

Traveler   : **And I have some laundry.**

                  Do you have laundry service?

Hotel Clerk: Of course. We'll come to your room to pick it up.

Traveler   : **Thanks. After breakfast, I will make a tour of the city.**

                  Make up my room, please.

Notes

▶ Can I have **an extra** blanket? (이불 **하나 더** 받을 수 있나요?)

        〃   **an extra** pillow? (베개 **하나 더**   〃   )

        〃   **some more** towels? (수건 **좀 더**   〃   )

▶ right away: 즉시 (= immediately)

▶ We'll **come** to your room to pick it up.

  (손님방으로 가지러 가겠습니다)

  상대가 있는 쪽으로 가는 것은 'go'가 아니라 'come'을 사용합니다.

▶ **make up:**

  ① (호텔에서) 침대 시트를 교환하거나 객실을 청소하고 정리 정돈하다

  ② 화해하다 (Let's make up. 화해합시다)

  ③ 보강하다 (I will make up the class tomorrow. 내일 수업 보강할게요)

  ④ 차지하다, 구성되다 (Girl students make up 60% of the class. 여학생이 학급
     의 60%를 차지합니다)

  ⑤ makeup: 화장 (She puts on a makeup everyday. 그녀는 매일 화장합니다)

대화 6. 서비스 요청/문의

여행자   : 여보세요. 203호입니다.
             이불 하나 더 받을 수 있을까요?
호텔 직원: 네. 즉시 갖다 드릴게요.
여행자   : 그리고 제가 세탁물이 좀 있는데요.
             세탁 서비스 되나요?
호텔 직원: 물론요. 세탁물 가지러 객실로 가겠습니다.
여행자   : 감사해요. 아침 식사 후 시내 관광을 하려 해요.
             방 청소 좀 부탁드립니다.

More Expressions

1. Can you call a taxi for me?
   (택시 좀 불러 주시겠어요?)

2. Do you have a pick-up service?
   (픽업 서비스가 되나요?)

3. Do you have a shuttle to the airport?
   (공항 가는 셔틀버스 있나요?)

4. I'd like a wake-up call at 7 tomorrow morning.
   (내일 아침 7시에 모닝콜 원합니다)
   ▶ 모닝콜은 영어로 'wake-up call'.

5. I'd like dinner in my room.
   I want dinner in my room.
   (제 방에서 저녁 식사를 하고 싶습니다)

6. I'd like to have my trousers washed.
   (바지를 세탁하고 싶습니다)
   ▶ 바지는 'trousers'로 항상 복수를 사용하며 'pants'라고도 함.

7. I'd like to have my blouse pressed.
   (제 블라우스를 다려 주세요)
   ▶ press = iron: 다림질하다

8. I'd like to have <u>my jacket</u> dry cleaned.

          <u>my dress shirt</u>

          <u>my suit</u>

(제 자켓/와이셔츠/양복을 드라이클리닝하고 싶습니다)

Notes

▶ 남성용 와이셔츠는 'shirt' 또는 'dress shirt'가 옳은 표현.

▶ 6, 7, 8번 문장은 주어+동사+목적어+목적보어(S+V+O+O.C) 형태로 5형식의 문장이며, have는 사역동사로 목적어가 wash 되고, press 되고, dry clean 되는 것이므로 수동의 의미가 있는 과거분사 'washed', 'pressed', 'dry cleaned'를 사용한 것.

Dialogue 7. 불편사항 요청

Hotel Clerk: Front desk. What can I do for you?
Traveler : **Hello. This is room 456.**
The toilet is clogged. Can you fix it?
Hotel Clerk: We will send someone up right away.
Traveler : **Thanks.**

Notes

▶ The toilet is clogged. (변기가 막혔어요.)
The sink 〃 (싱크대가 막혔어요.)
The drain 〃 (배수구가 막혔어요.)

대화 7. 불편사항 요청

호텔 직원: 프런트 데스크입니다. 무엇을 도와 드릴까요?
여행자 : **여보세요. 456호인데요.**
변기가 막혔어요. 고쳐 주시겠습니까?
호텔 직원: 사람을 즉시 보내 드리겠습니다.
여행자 : **감사해요.**

More Expressions

1. I'm locked out of my room.
   I locked myself out.
   I left my key in my room.
   (방 키를 방에 두고 나왔어요)

   The master key, please.
   (마스터키 부탁해요)

2. The shower doesn't work.
   (샤워기가 작동하지 않아요)

3. The bidet is not working.
   (비데가 작동하지 않아요)

4. Hot water is not coming out. (= There's no hot water)
   (뜨거운 물이 안 나와요)

   Cold water is not coming out. (= There's no cold water)
   (찬물이 안 나와요)

5. The toilet won't flush. (변기 물이 안 내려가요)
   * won't = will not

Dialogue 8. 숙소 체크아웃

Traveler   : **I'd like to check out.**
                   Here's my room key.

Hotel Clerk: I hope you enjoyed your stay here.
                   How would you like to pay?

Traveler   : **I'll pay by credit card.**
                   By the way, what's this charge for?

Hotel Clerk: It's for the mini-bar.

Traveler   : **I didn't use the mini-bar.**

Hotel Clerk: We'll check it.

Traveler   : **May I ask a favor of you?**
                   Would you keep my baggage until 5 p.m.?

Notes

▶ pay by credit card: 신용 카드로 지불하다
   pay in cash: 현금으로 지불하다

▶ May I ask a favor of you? (부탁 하나 드려도 될까요?)

대화 8. 숙소 체크아웃

여행자 : **체크아웃 하고 싶습니다. 여기 방 키 있습니다.**

호텔 직원: 편안하셨길 바랍니다. 어떻게 지불하시겠습니까?

여행자 : **신용카드로 할게요.**

　　　　　　그런데, 이건 무슨 비용이죠?

호텔 직원: 미니바 사용하신 겁니다.

여행자 : **전 미니바를 사용 안 했는데요.**

호텔 직원: 알아보겠습니다.

여행자 : **부탁 하나 드려도 될까요?**

　　　　　　제 짐을 오후 5시까지 보관해 주시겠어요?

Travel makes one modest.
You see what a tiny place you occupy in the world.

여행은 사람을 겸손하게 만든다. 세상에서 차지하고 있는 자신의 자리가
얼마나 작은 것인지 깨닫게 해준다.

- Gustave Flaubert -

Dialogue 1. 버스

1.

Traveler: Excuse me! Where is the bus stop?
And where can I get a ticket?

Lady　　: Go down this road about 100 meters.
It's in front of the First Bank.

2.

Traveler: Which bus goes to Central Park?

Man　　: You can take the bus no. 10.

Traveler: How many stops from here?

Notes

▶ 버스 정류장: bus stop

▶ 택시 승차장: taxi stand

▶ 기차역: train station/railway station/railroad station

▶ 전철역: subway station

3.

Traveler: A ticket to Central Park, please.
Give me the earliest ticket, please.

Staff　　: Okay.

Traveler: What's the fare?

Staff　　: It's 5 dollars.

Traveler: How long does it take to get there?

Staff　　: It will take about 10 minutes.

4.

Traveler: Do you go to Central Park?

Driver : Yes.

Traveler: Can you tell me where I should get off?

Driver : Okay. I will let you know when we get there.

대화 1. 버스

1.

여행자: 실례합니다! 버스정류장이 어디에 있나요?
그리고 어디서 티켓을 살 수 있죠?

숙녀 ：이 길로 약 100미터 정도 가시면 First Bank 앞에 있습니다.

2.

여행자: 어느 버스가 Central Park에 가나요?

남자 ：10번 버스 타시면 됩니다.

여행자: 여기서 몇 정거장이죠?

3.

여행자: Central Park 가는 표 한 장 부탁합니다.
가장 이른 표로 부탁해요.

직원 ：네.

여행자: 요금은 얼마예요?

직원 ：5불입니다.

여행자: 거기 가는 데 시간은 얼마나 걸립니까?

직원 ：약 10분 정도 걸릴 거예요.

4.

여행자: Central Park 가시나요?

운전사: 네.

여행자: 제가 어디서 내려야 하는지 말씀해 주시겠어요?

운전사: 네, 거기 도착하면 알려 드릴게요.

1. Where is the bus stop? (직접 의문문: 의문사 + 동사 + 주어)
   (버스 정류장이 어디에 있나요?)

   Do you know where the bus stop is?
   　　　　　(간접 의문문: 의문사 + 주어 + 동사)
   (버스 정류장이 어디에 있는지 아세요?)

   Can you tell me where the bus stop is?
   　　　　　(간접 의문문: 의문사 + 주어 + 동사)
   (버스 정류장이 어디에 있는지 말씀해 주시겠어요?)

   직접 의문문을 'Do you know'나 'Could you tell me' 뒤에 연결해 간접 의문문을 만드는 경우, know나 tell 동사의 목적어로 쓰이는 명사절 속에서는 의문사, 주어, 동사의 순으로 바뀌는 것에 유의하세요.

2. Which bus goes to Central Park?
   (어떤 버스가 Central Park에 갑니까?)

   Which bus should I take to go to Central Park?
   Which bus do I have to take to go to Central Park?
   (Central Park에 가려면 어느 버스를 타야 합니까?)

   '~해야 하다'의 뜻인 조동사 should, have to는 주어를 I로 하여 의문문을 만드는 경우, should I, do I have to로 표현합니다.

3. A ticket to Central Park, please.
   <u>I'd like</u> a ticket to Central Park.
   <u>I'd like to</u> get a ticket to Central Park.
   (Central Park 가는 표 한 장 부탁합니다)

   would like + 명사
   would like to + 동사

4. What's the fare?
   How much is the fare?

   '교통요금'은 fare를 사용합니다.
   what 대신 how much 사용 가능해요.

Dialogue 2. 택시

1.

Driver   : Where to, sir?

Traveler: Airport, please.

Driver   : Okay.

Traveler: Can you put this bag in the trunk?

Driver   : No problem.

Traveler: Please step on it. I'm in a hurry.

Driver   : I'd like to, but there's a lot of traffic.

Notes

▶ 남성에겐 Where to, sir?
  여성에겐 Where to, ma'am?

▶ Airport, please.
  To the airport, please.
  Please take me to the airport.
  (공항으로 가주세요)

▶ Please take me to this address.
  (이 주소로 가주세요)

▶ Hurry up, please.
  Make it quick, please.
  Step on it, please.
  (서둘러 주세요, 좀 빨리 부탁해요)

▶ There's a lot of traffic.
  There's a traffic jam.
  There's a traffic congestion.
  (차가 많이 막히네요)
  * traffic jam = traffic congestion (교통 혼잡)

대화 2. 택시

1.
운전사: 어디로 모실까요?
여행자: 공항 부탁합니다.
운전사: 알겠습니다.
여행자: 이 가방을 트렁크에 좀 넣어 주시겠어요?
운전사: 네.
여행자: 좀 밟아 주세요. 제가 좀 급해서요.
운전사: 그러고 싶은데, 차가 막히네요.

2.

Driver　: Where would you like to go?

Traveler: I'd like to go downtown.

....

Traveler: Where are we now?

Driver　: We are on King Street.

....

Traveler: Would you stop over there?

Driver　: OK. I'll drop you off in front of that building. Here we are.

Traveler: What's the fare?

Driver　: 17 dollars.

Traveler: Keep the change.

Notes

▶ Would you **stop** here?

　　　〃　　**pull over** here?

　　　〃　　**drop me off** here?

　　　〃　　**let me out** here?

위 문장 모두 '여기에서 내려주시겠어요?'라는 표현.
'here' 대신 'at the corner(코너에서)', 'past the next traffic light(다음 신호 지나서)',
'past the intersection(사거리 지나서)', 'in front of the post office(우체국 앞에서)'
등 구체적으로 표현할 수 있습니다.

2.

운전사: 어디 가길 원하세요?

여행자: 시내 가기 원합니다.

．．．．．．．．．．．．．．．．．．．．．．．

여행자: 여기가 어디죠?

운전사: King Street입니다.

．．．．．．．．．．．．．．．．．．．．．．．

여행자: 저기서 세워 주시겠어요?

운전사: 네. 저 건물 앞에서 내려 드릴게요. 다 왔습니다.

여행자: 요금이 얼마죠?

운전사: 17불입니다.

여행자: 잔돈은 괜찮습니다.

▶ '거리'를 뜻하는 다양한 단어

1. Street(St.): 동서 간을 잇는 시가지 도로

2. Avenue(Ave.): 남북 간을 잇는 시가지 도로

3. Boulevard(Blvd.): 도시를 가로지르거나 외곽의 대로

4. Drive(Dr.): 진입로, 구불구불한 도로

5. Road(Rd.): 두 지점을 연결하는 모든 종류의 길

6. alley: 골목길

7. no way out(= dead end): 막다른 길

Dialogue 3. 지하철

1.

Traveler: **Two tickets to National Museum, please.**

Staff　　: Here you are.

Traveler: **Which line goes to National Museum?**

Staff　　: Take line number 10.

2.

Traveler: **Oh, I got on the wrong train.**

Staff　　: What's your destination?

Traveler: **National Museum.**
Which stop should I get off at?

Staff　　: You should get off at City Hall and transfer to line number 3.

....

Traveler: **Where is the exit for National Museum?**

Staff　　: Take the exit number 7.

대화 3. 지하철

1.

여행자: 국립 박물관 가는 티켓 2장 부탁해요.

직원　: 여기 있습니다.

여행자: 국립 박물관엔 몇 호선이 가나요?

직원　: 10호선 타세요.

2.

여행자: 아, 열차를 잘못 탔어요.

직원　: 목적지가 어디세요?

여행자: 국립 박물관요.

　　　　제가 어느 역에서 내려야 하나요?

직원　: 시청역에서 내리셔서 3호선으로 갈아 타셔야 해요.

···

여행자: 국립 박물관으로 가는 출구가 어디인가요?

직원　: 7번 출구로 나가시면 됩니다.

Dialogue 4. 기차

1.

Traveler: A ticket to LA, please.

   When is the earliest train to LA?

Staff   : At 7:30 a. m.

Traveler: How often does the train run?

Staff   : Every 30 minutes.

Traveler: I'd like the 8 a. m. ticket, please.

2.

Traveler: Is this the right train for LA?

Staff   : Yes, you can take this.

Traveler: What time does the train leave?

Staff   : In 10 minutes.

Notes

▶ A ticket to LA, please.

 I'd like a ticket to LA. (would like + 명사)

 I'd like to get a ticket to LA. (would like to + 동사)

▶ When is the earliest train to LA?
 (LA 가는 가장 이른 기차는 언제 있나요?)

 When is the last train to LA?
 (LA가는 마지막 기차는 언제 있나요?)

 When is the next train to LA?
 (LA 가는 다음 기차는 언제 있나요?)

▶ In 10 minutes(10분 후예요) in + 시간 → '~후'라는 뜻이에요.

대화 4. 기차

1.

여행자: LA 가는 티켓 한 장 부탁해요.

　　　　LA 가는 가장 이른 기차는 언제 있나요?

직원　 : 오전 7시 30분요.

여행자: 기차는 얼마나 자주 운행되나요?

직원　 : 30분마다요.

여행자: 오전 8시 티켓 원합니다.

2.

여행자: 이거 LA 가는 기차 맞나요?

직원　 : 네, 이것 타시면 되어요.

여행자: 기차가 몇 시에 출발하나요?

직원　 : 10분 후예요.

Dialogue 5. 렌터카

1.

Traveler: Hi! I'd like to rent a car.

Staff　: What kind of car do you want?

Traveler: What kind of cars do you have?

Staff　: We have compact cars, mid-size cars, big cars, SUV, and even convertibles.

Traveler: I'd like an automatic SUV.

Staff　: How long do you want to use it?

Traveler: For a week.

Staff　: Can I see your passport and driver's license?

Traveler: Sure. Here you are.

Staff　: Fill in this form, please.

Notes

▶ compact car (소형차 = small car), mid-size car (중형차 = mid-sized car), big car (대형차 = full-size car, full-sized car)

▶ SUV: Sport Utility Vehicle (스포츠 실용차)

▶ convertible: ① 형용사) (다른 형태나 용도로) 전환 가능한
　　　　　　② 명사) 컨버터블 (지붕을 접었다 폈다, 또는 뗐다 붙였다 할 수 있는 승용차)

▶ fill in = fill out 작성하다

대화 5. 렌터카

1.

여행자: 안녕하세요? 자동차를 빌리고 싶습니다.

직원　: 어떤 종류의 차를 원하세요?

여행자: 어떤 종류의 차가 있나요?

직원　: 소형차, 중형차, 대형차, SUV, 컨버터블까지 있습니다.

여행자: 자동 SUV 원합니다.

직원　: 얼마 동안 사용하길 원하세요?

여행자: 1주일 동안요.

직원　: 여권과 운전 면허증을 좀 볼 수 있을까요?

여행자: 네, 여기 있어요.

직원　: 이 양식을 작성해 주세요.

2.

Traveler: What's the rental fee a day?

Staff　　: 120 dollars per day. Do you want insurance?

Traveler: Yes. I'd like full coverage, please.

　　　　　How much is insurance?

Staff　　: 30 dollars for a week.

Traveler: Do you offer GPS navigation?

Staff　　: Sure.

Traveler: Would you change the language setting to Korean?

Staff　　: Okay.

Traveler: I will take this car.

Notes

▶ a day = per day 하루에

▶ full coverage: 종합 보험, minimum coverage: 최소 보장보험

▶ What's the rental fee? = How much is the rental fee?

2.

여행자: 하루에 대여료가 얼마입니까?

직원　: 하루에 120불입니다. 보험 들기 원하십니까?

여행자: 네, 종합 보험 원합니다. 보험료는 얼마죠?

직원　: 1주에 30불입니다.

여행자: GPS 네비게이션 있나요?

직원　: 물론요.

여행자: 언어 세팅을 한국어로 해 주시겠어요?

직원　: 네.

여행자: 이 차로 하겠습니다.

Dialogue 6. 주유소

Traveler: We are running out of gas.
Is there a gas station nearby?

Lady   : Go straight about 200 meters.
And it'll be on your right.

Traveler: Thank you so much.

....

Staff   : How much gas would you like?

Traveler: Fill her up to 30 liters.

Staff   : Turn off the engine, please.

Notes

▶ We are running out of gas. (기름이 떨어져 가요)
= We are low on gas.

▶ 휘발유: (미국) gasoline 또는 gas, (영국) petrol
경유: diesel

▶ How much gas would you like?
= How much gas do you want?

▶ Fill her up, please. = Fill it up, please. (가득 넣어 주세요)
Fill her up to 30 liters. (30 리터 넣어 주세요)
Fill her up to 30 dollars. (30불 어치 넣어 주세요)

▶ turn off the engine: 시동을 끄다
start the engine: 시동을 걸다

대화 6. 주유소

여행자: 저희가 기름이 떨어져 가는데요.
**　　　　인근에 주유소 있나요?**
숙녀　: 약 200 미터 쭉 가시면 우측에 있을 거예요.
여행자: 대단히 감사합니다.
　　　　......................
직원　: 기름 얼마나 넣어 드릴까요?
여행자: 30 리터 넣어 주세요.
직원　: 엔진은 꺼 주세요.

Dialogue 7. 자동차 수리점

Traveler: Would you check my tires?
I think I have a flat tire.
Staff　　: Okay. Let me check.
Traveler: And the headlights are out.

Notes

▸ headlights: 전조등, taillights: 미등

대화 7. 자동차 수리점

여행자: 타이어 좀 점검해 주시겠어요?
타이어가 펑크가 난 것 같아요.
직원　　: 네, 점검해 볼게요.
여행자: 그리고 전조등도 나갔어요.

* 자동차에 문제가 있을 때의 다양한 표현

1. Would you check the tires?
    "   "   the engine oil?
    "   "   the air conditioner?
    "   "   the GPS navigation?
   (타이어/엔진오일/에어컨/네비게이션 좀 점검해 주시겠어요?)

2. Would you ~
   Could you ~
   Can you ~
   Will you ~

   위 모두 you를 주어로 해서 '상대방에게 요청할 때' 쓰는 표현입니다.
   Would you, Could you가 Can you, Will you 보다 더 공손한 표현입니다.

3. The brake doesn't work.
   The air conditioner doesn't work.
   The GPS navigation doesn't work.
   (브레이크/에어컨/네비게이션이 작동을 안 합니다)

4. The battery is dead.
   The battery is out.
   (배터리가 나갔어요)

Dialogue 8. 교통사고

Traveler: Hello, is this the police station?
         I had a car accident.

Police   : Where are you now?

Traveler: We are on Pine Street.

         ………………………

Police   : How did it happen?

Traveler: I got rear-ended.

Police   : Is anybody hurt?

Traveler: I sprained my neck. I can't move it.

Police   : Oh, that's too bad. I will take you to the hospital.

Traveler: Thanks.

Police   : Do you have any insurance?

Traveler: Yes, I have travel insurance.
         I will call my car rental company.

Police   : I will call a tow truck.

Notes

▸ I will **call** my car rental company. (렌터카 회사에 전화할게요)
  : (call: **전화하다**)

  I will **call** a tow truck. (제가 견인차를 부를게요)
  : (call: **부르다**)

대화 8. 교통사고

여행자: 여보세요? 거기 경찰서죠? 차 사고가 났습니다.

경찰 : 지금 어디신가요?

여행자: Pine Street에 있어요.

....

경찰 : 어떻게 된 거예요?

여행자: 추돌 당했어요.

경찰 : 다친 사람 있나요?

여행자: 제가 목을 삐었어요. 움직일 수가 없네요.

경찰 : 오, 안됐군요. 병원에 데려다 드릴게요.

여행자: 고맙습니다.

경찰 : 보험에 가입하셨나요?

여행자: 네, 여행자 보험 들었어요. 제 렌터카 회사에 연락할게요.

경찰 : 저는 견인차를 부르겠습니다.

Dialogue 9. 교통 위반

Police : May I see your driver's license?

Traveler: What's the problem, officer?

Police : You made an illegal U turn.

Traveler: I didn't know it's illegal.

Police : I'm going to give you a ticket.

Traveler: I'm a tourist.

Please give me a break.

Police : Sorry.

Traveler: How much is the fine?

Police : It'll be 250 dollars.

Notes

▶ illegal: 불법적인 ↔ legal: 합법적인

▶ I'm going to give you a ticket. : 딱지 떼겠습니다.

▶ give someone a break: ~에게 기회를 주다, 너그럽게 봐주다

▶ fine: 명사) 벌금

▶ You were speeding. (과속하셨어요)

▶ You ignored the stop sign. (정지신호를 무시하셨어요)

▶ I almost got a ticket. (거의 딱지 뗄 뻔했네요)

대화 9. 교통 위반

경찰　 : 운전 면허증 좀 보여 주시겠어요?
여행자: 경관님, 무엇이 문제인가요?
경찰　 : 불법 유턴을 하셨어요.
여행자: 불법인 줄 몰랐습니다.
경찰　 : 딱지를 끊겠습니다.
여행자: 저 관광객인데요.
　　　　한번 봐주세요.
경찰　 : 미안합니다.
여행자: 벌금은 얼마죠?
경찰　 : 250불입니다.

We live in a wonderful world
that is full of beauty, charm, and adventure.
There is no end to the adventures we can have
if only we seek them with our eyes open.

우리는 아름답고 매력적이고 모험으로 가득 찬 멋진 세상에 살고 있다.

우리가 눈을 뜨고 찾기만 하면 우리가 할 수 있는 모험은 끝이 없다.

- Jawaharial Nehru -

Dialogue 1. 예약

Traveler: I'd like to reserve a table for 7 o'clock tonight.

Waiter : I'm afraid we are fully booked at that time.

Traveler: How about tomorrow?

Waiter : No problem. How many are there in your party?

Traveler: There are four of us.

Waiter : Could I have your name and phone number?

Traveler: Heeseong Yoon. 82-10-0000-0000.

Waiter : Thank you for calling, sir.

> Notes

▶ reserve = book (예약하다)

▶ How about ~ = What about ~ (~는 어때요?)

▶ How many in your party?

  How many are there in your party? (일행이 몇 분이세요?)

  * party: ① 파티 (have/hold/throw a party 파티를 열다)

      ② 일행

      ③ political party: 정당

      (ruling party: 여당, opposition party: 야당)

▶ May I ~, Can I ~, Could I ~

  모두 주어를 I로 해서 '내가 허락을 구할 때' 쓸 수 있는 표현으로 Could I가 May I, Can I보다 더 공손한 표현.

▶ 82-10-0000-0000: 82는 한국 국가번호이고, 국제전화 시 휴대폰 번호 010-0000-0000에서 첫 숫자 0은 생략.

대화 1. 예약

여행자: 오늘 밤 7시에 테이블 하나 예약하고 싶습니다.

웨이터: 그 시간엔 예약이 꽉 찼습니다.

여행자: 내일은 어때요?

웨이터: 문제없어요. 일행이 몇 분이세요?

여행자: 저희 4명이에요.

웨이터: 성함과 전화번호는요?

여행자: 윤희성이고요. 82-10-0000-0000입니다.

웨이터: 전화 주셔서 감사합니다.

Dialogue 2. 식당에서

1. 도착

Traveler: We have a reservation at 7 o'clock.

Waiter　: May I have your name?

Traveler: Heeseong Yoon.

Waiter　: This way, please. Let me show you to your table.

Traveler: If possible, I'd like to sit by the window.

Notes

▶ I'd like to sit by the window. (창가로 앉고 싶습니다)

　　〃　　in the corner. (코너에 앉고 싶습니다)

　Any table will be fine. (아무 테이블이나 괜찮아요)

▶ cafeteria　: 학교나 직장의 구내식당 같은 셀프 서비스 식당

　bistro　　: 간단한 식사를 할 수 있는 작은 식당

　restaurant: 테이블에 앉아 서비스를 받을 수 있는 식당

　　　　　　반드시 입구에서 웨이터가 안내해 줄 때까지 기다리는 것이 예의이
　　　　　　며, 고급 레스토랑의 경우는 격식에 맞지 않은 옷차림이면 입장이 불
　　　　　　가할 수 있으니 예약 시 미리 복장규칙(dress code)을 물어보는 것이
　　　　　　좋음

대화 2. 식당에서

1. 도착

여행자: 저희 7시 예약한 거 있는데요.

웨이터: 성함이 어떻게 되시죠?

여행자: 윤희성입니다.

웨이터: 이쪽으로 오세요. 손님 테이블로 안내해 드리겠습니다.

여행자: 가능하다면, 창가로 앉고 싶습니다.

2. 메뉴판

Traveler: I'd like the menu, please.

Waiter : Can I take your order?

Traveler: Can you wait for a minute?

We haven't decided yet.

Waiter : Take your time. I'll come back.

Notes

▶ Menu, please. (메뉴 부탁해요.)

I'd like the menu, please.

▶ Can I take your order? (주문받아도 될까요?)

Are you ready to order? (주문하실 준비 되셨어요?)

Would you like to order? (주문하시겠어요?)

▶ for a minute = for a moment = for a second (잠시만)

2. 메뉴판

여행자: 메뉴 부탁합니다.

웨이터: 주문 받을까요?

여행자: 잠시 기다려 주시겠어요?

저희가 아직 결정하지 못했어요.

웨이터: 천천히 보세요. 다시 오겠습니다.

3. 주문

Traveler: What's good here?

What do you recommend?

Waiter : How about sirloin steak?

Traveler: OK. I'll have that.

Waiter : How would you like your steak?

Traveler: Medium, please.

Waiter : Anything to drink?

Traveler: I'd like a glass of red wine.

Waiter : Is that all?

Traveler: That's all for now.

Notes

▶ Is that all? (그게 전부인가요?)

Anything else? (더 필요한 거 있으세요?)

3. 주문

여행자: 여기 무얼 잘하나요?

　　　　　무엇을 추천해 주시겠어요?

웨이터: 등심 스테이크 어때요?

여행자: 좋아요. 그것으로 하죠.

웨이터: 스테이크는 어떻게 해드릴까요?

여행자: 중간 익힘으로 해주세요.

웨이터: 음료는요?

여행자: 레드 와인 한잔하고 싶어요.

웨이터: 다 주문하셨나요?

여행자: 지금으로선 그게 다입니다.

4. 후식

Waiter : How did you like your steak?

Was it to your taste?

Traveler 1: It was excellent. I really enjoyed it.

Waiter : Good to hear that.

Would you like some dessert?

Traveler 1: What do you have for dessert?

Waiter : We have coffee, tea, and some ice cream.

Traveler 1: I'll have a scoop of vanilla ice cream.

Traveler 2: I will skip dessert.

Notes

▶ dessert: 후식, desert: 명사) 사막, 동사) 저버리다

▶ I will skip dessert. = I will pass dessert.

---

4. 후식

웨이터 : 스테이크 맛이 어떠셨어요?

입맛에 맞으셨나요?

여행자 1: 훌륭했어요. 정말 맛있게 먹었습니다.

웨이터 : 그렇게 말씀하시니 기쁘네요.

후식 좀 드시겠어요?

여행자 1: 후식으로 뭐가 있나요?

웨이터 : 커피, 홍차, 아이스크림이 있어요.

여행자 1: 바닐라 아이스크림 한 스쿱 주세요.

여행자 2: 전 디저트 안 먹을래요.

More Expressions

1. My order hasn't come out yet.
   (주문한 게 아직 안 나왔어요)

2. Would you put a rush on my order?
   (제가 주문한 것 좀 서둘러 주시겠어요?)

3. I've been waiting for thirty minutes.
   (30분이나 기다리고 있습니다)

4. How **would you like** your steak?
   (스테이크를 **어떻게 해드릴까요?**/얼마나 익혀 드릴까요?)

   Well-done, please. (완전 익힘 부탁해요)
   Medium, please. (중간 익힘)
   Rare, please. (살짝만 익힘)
   Medium well-done, please. (미디엄과 웰던 사이로 익힘)
   Medium rare, please. (미디엄과 레어 사이로 익힘)

5. How **do you like** your steak?

   A. 일반적으로 **어떻게 하는 스테이크를 좋아하세요?**
      I like well-done. (저는 웰던을 좋아해요)
      I like medium. (저는 미디엄을 좋아해요)
   B. **스테이크 맛이 어떠세요?**
      Pretty good. Fantastic. So delicious. (아주 맛있어요)
      Too tough. (너무 질겨요)
      Terrible. Awful. (형편없어요)

It's undercooked. (덜 익었어요)
It's overcooked. (너무 익었어요)

6. How would you like your coffee?
(커피를 어떻게 해드릴까요?)

With sugar, please. (설탕을 넣어 주세요)
With cream, please. (크림)
With sugar and cream, please. (설탕과 크림)
Black, please. (블랙으로 주세요)

7. How would you like your eggs?
(계란을 어떻게 해드릴까요?)

Sunny-side up, please.
Scrambled, please.

```
┌─ Fried      ┌─ Over easy
│             ├─ Over medium
│             ├─ Over hard
│             └─ Sunnyside up
├─ Scrambled
├─ Boiled     ┌─ Hard boiled
│             └─ Soft boiled
└─ Poached
```

Notes

▶ fried egg: 계란프라이
 - over easy, over medium, over hard:
  계란프라이를 양쪽 다 익힘 정도에 따라 표현한 것
 - sunny-side up: 계란프라이를 뒤집지 않고 한쪽만 익히는 것
▶ scrambled: 계란을 풀어 우유와 버터를 넣고 섞은 후 팬에 볶는 것

▶ boiled: 삶은 계란

　hard boiled: 완숙, soft boiled: 반숙

▶ poached: 수란. 국자처럼 만든 수란기에 계란을 깨트려 넣은 후 흩트리지 않고
뜨거운 물에 넣어 익힌 것

8. Would you like <u>some more coffee?</u>

　　　　　　　some more beer?

　　　　　　　some more wine?

　　　　　　　(커피/맥주/와인을 좀 더 드시겠어요?)

9. I'd like a glass of red wine. (레드 와인 한 잔)

　　〃　　a glass of white wine. (화이트 와인 한 잔)

　I'd like a bottle of red wine. (레드 와인 한 병)

　　〃　　a bottle of white wine. (화이트 와인 한 병)

　I'd like a can of beer. (맥주 한 캔)

　　〃　　a bottle of beer. (맥주 한 병)

10. I dropped my fork. (제 포크/스푼/나이프를 떨어뜨렸어요)

　　〃　　my spoon.

　　〃　　my knife.

　Can I have one more fork? (포크/스푼/나이프 하나 더 주실래요?)

　　〃　　one more spoon?

　　〃　　one more knife?

11. Can I have some more sauce? (소스/냅킨 좀 더 주실래요?)

　　〃　　some more napkins?

141

*The real voyage of discovery
consists not in seeking new landscapes,
but in having new eyes.*

여행의 진정한 발견은 새로운 풍경을 찾는 게 아니라
새로운 시각을 갖게 되는 것이다.

- Marcel Proust -

Dialogue 1. 단품

Staff : Can I take your order?

Traveler: I'd like a hamburger and French fries.

Staff : What size would you like?

Traveler: Medium, please.

Staff : For here or to go?

Traveler: To go, please.

Notes

▶ hamburger = burger (햄버거)

▶ French fries = fries (감자튀김)(미국), chips(영국)

대화 1. 단품

직원 : 주문하시겠어요?

여행자: 햄버거 하나와 감자튀김 원해요.

직원 : 어떤 사이즈를 원하세요?

여행자: 미디엄요.

직원 : 여기서 드시겠어요, 아니면 갖고 가실 건가요?

여행자: 갖고 갈 거예요.

Dialogue 2. 세트 메뉴

Traveler: **I will have the combo number 2.**

Staff　　 : For here or to go?

Traveler: **For here, please.**

Staff　　 : Do you want that with everything?

Traveler: **Hold the onions and take it easy on the mustard.**
　　　　　 And I'll have a Coke with no ice.

Notes

▶ combo: 세트 메뉴.
　(비격식) 여러 종류의 요리를 섞어서 제공하는 음식 이름에 쓰임.

▶ Hold the onions, please. = No onions, please. (양파는 빼 주세요)
　Hold: ① 잡다, 쥐다 (Hold my hand. - 제 손을 잡으세요)
　　　　② (명령문 형태로) 중단하라 (Hold the fire! - 사격 중지!)
　　　　③ (비격식)(명령문 형태로) 넣지 말아요.
　　　　　 Give me a hot dog, but hold the mayo.
　　　　　 (핫도그 하나 주시는데요, 마요네즈는 빼 주세요)

▶ Take it easy on the mustard. = Go easy on the mustard.
　(겨자는 조금만 넣어 주세요)

▶ No ice, please. = With no ice, please. = Without ice, please.
　(얼음은 넣지 마세요)

대화 2. 세트 메뉴

여행자: 세트 메뉴 2번 먹을게요.

직원　: 여기서 드시겠어요, 아니면 갖고 가실 건가요?

여행자: 여기서 먹을게요.

직원　: 모두 다 넣어 드릴까요?

여행자: 양파는 빼주시고요, 겨자는 조금만 넣어 주세요.
그리고 콜라는 얼음 넣지 말아 주세요.

I have promises to keep, and miles to go before I sleep.

나에겐 지켜야 할 약속이 있고, 잠들기 전에 가야 할 길이 있다.

- Robert Frost -

커피숍/맥주집/와인바

Dialogue 1. 커피숍

1.

Staff : Can I take your order? What would you like?

Traveler: I'd like one americano, please.

Staff : Hot or iced?

Traveler: Iced, please.

Staff : For here or to go?

Traveler: For here, please.

Staff : What size do you want?

Traveler: Make it small, and just one shot, please.

Notes

▸ Hot, please. ↔ Iced, please.

▸ Small, please. = Short, please.

　Medium, please. = Regular, please. = Tall, please. = Normal, please.

　Large, please. = Grande, please. (Grande: 그란데. large를 의미하는 스페인어)

▸ shot: ① 총기 발사, 발포

　　　 ② 사진

　　　 ③ 주사 (한 대)

　　　 ④ (특히 독한 술) 한 잔, 한 모금

　　　 ⑤ 커피 원액

　　　　 (Please add one more shot. 샷 하나 더 넣어 주세요)

대화 1. 커피숍

1.

직원　: 주문 받을까요? 무얼 드시겠어요?

여행자: 아메리카노 한 잔 주세요.

직원　: 뜨겁게 해 드릴까요, 차게 해 드릴까요?

여행자: 차게 해 주세요.

직원　: 여기서 드세요, 가지고 가세요?

여행자: 여기서요.

직원　: 어떤 사이즈로 하시겠어요?

여행자: 작은 걸로 주시고요, 샷은 하나만 넣어 주세요.

2.

Staff   : Can I take your order?

Traveler: One small cappuccino for here, please.

Staff   : Do you want whipped cream on top?

Traveler: Go easy on the foam, please.

Staff   : It'll be ready in a few minutes.

▶ One small cappuccino 뒤에 for here나 to go를 붙여서 한 문장으로 표현 가능.

　One small cappuccino to go, please.
　One small cappuccino for here, please.

▶ Do you want ~ = Would you like ~

▶ No whipped cream, please. (휘핑크림은 넣지 말아 주세요)
　Go easy on whipped cream, please.
　Take it easy on whipped cream, please.
　(휘핑크림은 조금만 넣어 주세요)

　A lot of whipped cream, please. (휘핑크림 많이 넣어 주세요)

▶ in a few minutes = in a few moments = in a few seconds
　(잠시 후에)

2.

직원　: 주문하시겠어요?

여행자: 카푸치노 작은 사이즈로 여기서 마실 거예요.

직원　: 위에 휘핑크림 올려 드릴까요?

여행자: 거품 약간만 얹어 주세요.

직원　: 잠시 후면 준비될 겁니다.

Dialogue 2. 맥주집

Staff　　: What would you like?

Traveler 1: What kind of beers do you have?

Staff　　: We have Budweiser, Heineken, and stout.

Traveler 1: Let me have a bottle of stout.

Traveler 2: Do you have draft beer?

Staff　　: Yes.

Traveler 2: I will have a glass of draft beer.

....

Traveler 1: Excuse me. I don't think we ordered this.

Staff　　: It's on the house.

Traveler 1: Oh, thank you.

Notes

▶ stout: 흑맥주
▶ draft beer: 생맥주

▶ a bottle of stout: 흑맥주 한 병
　a can of beer: 맥주 한 캔
　a glass of draft beer: 생맥주 한 잔
　a pitcher of draft beer: 생맥주 한 피처
　* pitcher: 귀 모양의 손잡이와 주둥이가 있는 생맥주 담는 용기

▶ have: 먹다, 마시다 (eat, drink 모두 포함하는 단어)
▶ It's on the house.
　It's free.
　It's complimentary. (그건 서비스예요/그건 무료예요)

대화 2. 맥주집

직원　　: 뭐 드시겠어요?

여행자 1: 어떤 종류의 맥주가 있나요?

직원　　: 버드와이저, 하이네켄, 그리고 흑맥주가 있어요.

여행자 1: 전 흑맥주 한 병 마실게요.

여행자 2: 생맥주도 있으신가요?

직원　　: 네.

여행자 2: 전 생맥주 한 잔 할게요.

....

여행자 1: 실례지만 저희 이거 안 시킨 것 같은데요.

직원　　: 그건 서비스예요.

여행자 1: 아, 감사합니다.

Dialogue 3. 위스키/와인바

Staff : What would you like to drink?

Traveler 1: Can you recommend a popular wine?

Staff : How about Chilean red wine?

Traveler 1: OK. I'll try that.

Traveler 2: I'd like a whisky.

Staff : On the rocks?

Traveler 2: Yes, please.

Can I order it by the glass?

Staff : Of course.

Traveler 1: This really hits the spot.

Notes

▶ On the rocks? (얼음 넣어 드릴까요?)

Yes, please. (네)

No, straight, please. (아니오, 넣지 말아주세요)

* straight: ① 곧은, 똑바른

② 솔직한, 정직한

③ (술) 아무것도 타지 않은 (스트레이트의)

▶ dry wine: 달지 않은 와인, sweet wine: 달콤한 와인

sparkling wine: 기포와 거품을 가지고 있는 와인

▶ May I propose a toast **to** <u>our health</u>? (우리의 건강)

〃 **to** <u>our happiness</u>? (우리의 행복)

〃 **to** <u>our friendship</u>? (우리의 우정)

〃 **to** <u>our love</u>? (우리의 사랑)

= I'd like to propose a toast to our health.

(우리의 건강을 위하여 건배제의 하겠습니다)

▶ Cheers! = Bottoms up! (건배!) = Salud! (스페인어로 건배!)

156

대화 3. 위스키/와인바

직원　　 : 무엇을 마시고 싶으세요?

여행자 1: 유명한 와인 하나 추천해 주시겠어요?

직원　　 : 칠레 레드 와인 어떠세요?

여행자 1: 한번 마셔 볼게요.

여행자 2: 저는 위스키로 하겠어요.

직원　　 : 얼음 넣어 드릴까요?

여행자 2: 네. 잔으로 시켜도 될까요?

직원　　 : 물론입니다.

여행자 1: 이 와인 정말 끝내 주네요.

Dialogue 4. 계산

Traveler 1: Check, please. How much is it altogether?

Staff　　: The total comes to 90 dollars.

Traveler 2: Let's go Dutch.

Traveler 1: Don't worry. It's on me.

Staff　　: Would you sign here?

Traveler 1: OK. Can I have the receipt?

Staff　　: Here it is.

Notes

▶ Check, please. = Bill, please.

　I'd like the check, please. = I'd like the bill, please.

▶ Separate checks, please. (각자 따로 계산해 주세요)

▶ come to ~: ~에 달하다

▶ **제가 낼게요**

　1) **It's on me.** (그거 제가 낼게요)

　　Lunch/Dinner is on me. (점심/저녁 제가 냅니다)

　　Coffee is on me. (커피 제가 냅니다)

　2) **You are my guest today.** (당신은 오늘 제 손님이세요)

　3) **Let me take care of it.** (제가 처리 할게요/제가 낼게요)

▶ **각자 냅시다**

　1) **Let's go Dutch.** (각자 내어요)

　2) **Let's go fifty fifty.** (반반 내어요)

　3) **Let's split the bill.** (나누어서 계산합시다)

대화 4. 계산

여행자 1: 계산서 부탁해요. 모두 얼마인가요?

직원　　: 전부 90불입니다.

여행자 2: 각자 냅시다.

여행자 1: 걱정 마세요. 제가 냅니다.

직원　　: 여기 서명해 주시겠어요?

여행자 1: 네. 영수증 받을 수 있을까요?

직원　　: 여기 있습니다.

'Let's go Dutch'의 유래

1602년 네덜란드는 아시아지역에 대한 식민지 경쟁과 무역을 위해 동인도 회사를 세우고 영국과 식민지 경쟁에 나섰습니다. 17C 후반, 3차례에 걸친 영국-네덜란드 전쟁으로 서로 갈등이 이어졌답니다. 이에 영국인들이 Dutch(네덜란드의/ 네덜란드인/네덜란드어)라는 단어를 부정적으로 사용하게 되었습니다.

예)
Dutch courage: 맨 정신에 낼 수 없어 술을 빌어 내는 용기
Dutch treat: 가짜 대접. 자기 것 자기가 내는 대접 아닌 대접

Dutch pay는 잘못된 표현이고 Dutch treat이 옳은 표현임.
(Let's drink on a Dutch treat. 돈을 추렴해서 한잔합시다)

Do not go where the path may lead;
go instead where there is no path and leave a trail.

길이 이끄는 대로 가지 말고,

대신 길이 없는 곳으로 가서 자취를 남겨라.

- Ralph Waldo Emerson -

Dialogue 1. 옷가게

1. 둘러볼 때

Staff　　: Can I help you?

Traveler: No, thanks. I'm just looking.

Staff　　: Take your time, and let me know if you need any help.

Notes

▶ I'm just looking.

I'm just looking around.

I'm just browsing.

(그냥 둘러보는 중이에요)

대화 1. 옷가게

1. 둘러볼 때
직원　: 도와 드릴까요?
여행자: 아니오. 그냥 둘러보는 중이에요.
직원　: 천천히 보시고, 도움 필요하시면 말씀하세요.

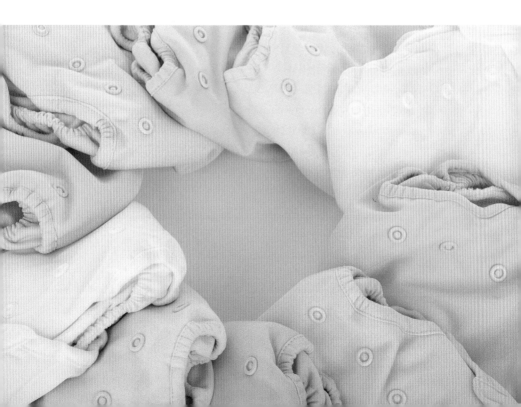

2. 구입

Traveler: Can I try this on?

Staff　　: Sure.

Traveler: Where's the dressing room?

Staff　　: The fitting room is over there.

....

Staff　　: Wow, it looks good on you!
　　　　　How do you like it?

Traveler: Thanks! But it's a little loose under the arms.
Do you have this in a smaller size?

Staff　　: Yes.

Traveler: Is this machine-washable?

Staff　　: Yes, it is.

Traveler: Good. I will take this. I want to buy one more for my sister,
and I'd like it gift-wrapped.

Staff　　: Okay.

Notes

▸ May I try **them** on?: 안경, 귀고리, 바지, 구두처럼 쌍을 이루는 복수인 경우
　May I try **it** on?: 셔츠, 자켓, 블라우스 등 단수인 경우

▸ dressing room = fitting room = changing room (탈의실)

▸ It looks good on you. (그것 당신에게 잘 어울리네요)

Your jacket **looks** good on you.
Your shirt　　　　〃

Your pants **look** good on you.
Your glasses　　　〃

164

2. 구입

여행자: 이거 입어 봐도 될까요?

직원　：물론요.

여행자: 탈의실이 어디인가요?

직원　：탈의실은 저쪽이에요.

....

직　원: 와우, 잘 어울리세요. 손님은 어떠세요?

여행자: 고마워요. 그런데 제 팔 안쪽이 약간 헐렁해요.
　　　　이거 더 작은 사이즈로 있나요?

직원　：네.

여행자: 이거 세탁기로 빨아도 되나요?

직원　：네.

여행자: 좋네요. 저 이것으로 할게요. 제 여동생을 위해
　　　　하나 더 샀으면 하는데 선물용으로 포장해 주세요.

직원　：그러죠.

3. 계산

Traveler: Can you give me a discount?

Staff　　: That's a good buy. That's a steal.

Traveler: That's out of my price range.

Staff　　: What's your price range?

Traveler: 100 dollars.

Staff　　: I will give you a 5% discount.
　　　　　　That's my last offer.

Traveler: OK. I'll take it.
　　　　　Can I pay in installments?

Staff　　: Sure. How many installments?

Traveler: Six months, please.

Staff　　: Okay. Signature, please.

Notes

▸ That's a good buy. (잘 사시는 겁니다)
　That's a good price. (좋은 가격이에요)

▸ steal: ① 동사) 훔치다
　　　　② 명사) 횡재, 공짜나 다름없이 산 물건
　　　　③ 명사) (야구) 도루

▸ I'd like to pay in installments.
　(할부로 지불하고 싶어요)

▸ I'd like to pay in a lump sum.
　= I'd like to pay in full.
　(일시불로 지불하고 싶어요)

3. 계산

여행자: 깎아 주시겠어요?

직원　: 잘 사시는 겁니다. 거저예요.

여행자: 제 가격대를 벗어났어요.

직원　: 생각하시는 가격대가 어떻게 되세요?

여행자: 100불요.

직원　: 5% 할인해 드릴게요.
　　　　제 마지막 제안입니다.

여행자: 좋아요, 그걸로 할게요.
　　　　제가 할부로 지불할 수 있을까요?

직원　: 물론요. 몇 개월 할부요?

여행자: 6개월요.

직원　: 알았어요. 서명 부탁합니다.

1. May I help you? (도와 드릴까요?)
   Can I help you?
   How can I help you?
   What can I do for you?

2. Yes, please. I'm looking for a shirt.
   Would you show me the shirt over there?
   (네, 셔츠를 찾고 있어요. 저기 있는 셔츠 좀 보여주시겠어요?)

   No, thanks. I'm just looking (around).
              I'm just browsing.
   (아뇨, 그냥 둘러보는 중이에요)

   Notes
   ▶ look at: 보다
   ▶ look for: 찾다
   ▶ look around: 둘러보다
   ▶ look after: 돌보다

3. It's too loose for me. (제게 너무 헐렁해요)
   It's too tight for me. (제게 너무 꽉 껴요)

   It's a little loose for me. (제게 조금 헐렁해요)
   It's a little tight for me. (제게 조금 꽉 껴요)

4. Do you have this <u>in a smaller size</u>? (더 작은 사이즈 있나요?)

                in a larger size? (더 큰 사이즈 있나요?)

                <u>in a different color</u>? (다른 색상으로 있나요?)

                in blue? (파란색으로 있나요?)

                <u>in any other style</u>? (다른 스타일로 있나요?)

5. I'd like a darker/lighter color.
(더 짙은/옅은 색으로 원합니다)

6. Do you have anything <u>similar that's less expensive</u>?
(비슷한 것으로 더 저렴한 것 있나요?)

Do you have anything <u>cheaper</u>?
(더 싼 것 있나요?)

Do you have anything <u>of higher quality</u>?
(더 품질 좋은 것 있나요?)

7. That's too <u>expensive</u>. (너무 비싸요)
           much.

8. I like it very much. (아주 맘에 들어요)
That's just what I wanted. (제가 바로 원하던 것입니다)

This isn't exactly what I wanted.
(제가 원하던 것과 똑같은 것은 아닌데요)

9. I think this color/style doesn't suit me well.
   (이 색상/스타일은 저와 잘 맞지 않는 것 같아요)

10. May I try this on? (이것 입어 봐도 되나요?)
              that
              it
              them

11. It's too big. (너무 커요)
       kind of tight. (다소 조이는데요)
       very becoming. (잘 어울립니다)
       too loud for my tastes. (제 취향에는 너무 야한데요)

▶ a kind of: 일종의
  kind of: 다소
▶ becoming: 형용사) 어울리는

12. The sleeves are too long. (소매가 너무 길어요)
    Can you alter this for me? (이것 좀 고쳐주시겠어요?)

13. One size fits all. (프리 사이즈입니다)

14. Can you give me a discount? (좀 깎아 주시겠어요?)
              come down a little?
              cut down the price a little?
              lower the price?
    It's a fixed price. (정찰제입니다)
    The price is fixed.

15. This is a good buy. (잘 사시는 겁니다)

16. That's a rip-off. (바가지 썼어요)

17. Do you take credit cards? (신용카드 받으시죠?)

            accept traveler's checks? (여행자 수표 받으시나요?)

18. I'll pay in cash. (현금으로 지불하겠습니다)

        by credit card. (신용카드로)

        by traveler's check. (여행자 수표로)

19. Can I pay in installments? (할부로 지불할 수 있나요?)

20. Can I get a refund on this? (이거 환불받을 수 있나요?)

21. Can I get a tax refund on this?
   (이거 세금환급 받을 수 있나요?)

공항이나 기내에서 면세품을 구매할 수 있지만, 외국 상점에서 구입한 물건을 한국으로 갖고 들어오는 경우도 출국 전에 현지 공항에서 부가세를 환급받을 수 있습니다. 이를 위해선 Tax Free(Refund) Shopping 사인이 있는 상점에서 물건을 구입해야 하고, 계산 시 직원에게 'Can I get a tax refund on this?'라고 물어보아 환급 전표(Refund cheque)를 받습니다. 그 후 공항의 Tax Refund Office에서 세금을 환급받을 수 있습니다.

※ 의류 사이즈 비교

한국 (1)	44	55	66	77	88
한국 (2)	85	90	95	100	105
미국	2	4-6	8-10	12-14	16-18
	XS	S	M	L	XL
유럽	36	38-40	42-44	46-48	48-50

Dialogue 2. 마트

1. 장소 묻기

Traveler: Where is the grocery store?

Lady   : Go down this street for two blocks.

           And it'll be between the bank and the post office.

Traveler: Is it within walking distance?

           How long will it take to get there?

Lady   : It's about a five-minute walk.

Traveler: Thanks a lot.

Notes

▶ grocery store: 식료품점

▶ It's about a five-minute walk. (걸어서 약 5분 거리예요)

  = It takes about five minutes on foot.

  It's about a five-minute drive. (차로 5분 거리예요)

  = It takes about five minutes by car.

* 위에서 walk나 drive는 명사로 쓰인 것이므로 관사 'a'를 붙이며, 이때 five-minute은 five와 minute 사이에 '짧은 줄표(-)'를 넣고 minute 다음엔 's'를 붙이지 않는 것에 유의하세요.

대화 2. 마트

1. 장소 묻기

여행자: 식료품점이 어디에 있습니까?

숙녀　: 이 길로 두 블록 가세요.

　　　　그러면 은행과 우체국 사이에 있을 거예요.

여행자: 거기 걸어가도 되나요?

**　　　　거기 가는 데 시간이 얼마나 걸릴까요?**

숙녀　: 도보로 5분 거리입니다.

여행자: 감사해요.

2. 마트 안에서

Traveler: Where are the dairy products?

Staff   : They are in aisle 7.

....

Traveler: Do you have fat-free yogurt?

Staff   : I think we're out of that item.

Traveler: I'll buy this blueberry yogurt.

Staff   : Buy two and get one free.

Notes

▶ dairy products: 유제품
▶ aisle: ① 통로
      ② 마트에서 각종 코너(과일 코너, 와인 코너…)는
        corner라 하지 않고 aisle이라 함

▶ fat-free yogurt: 지방 없는 요거트
▶ free: ① 형용사) 자유로운, 무료의, ~이 없는
      ② 부사) 무료로
        (Buy two and get one free.: 두 개 사면 한 개 공짜)
      ③ 동사) 자유케 하다, 석방하다, 풀어 주다

▶ We're out of that item. (그 물건 떨어졌어요)
   It's out of stock. (재고가 없어요)

▶ **Buy one get one.** (BOGO)
   Buy one get one free.
   Buy one take one free.
   (한 개 사면 한 개 공짜입니다)

2. 마트 안에서

여행자: 유제품은 어디에 있죠?

직원   : 7번 코너에 있어요.

....

여행자: 무지방 요거트 있나요?

직원   : 그 제품은 떨어졌는데요.

여행자: 이 블루베리 요거트로 사겠습니다.

직원   : 두 개 사시면 하나는 공짜입니다.

1. Where is the grocery store?
   (직접 의문문: 의문사+동사+주어)

   Can you tell me where the grocery store is?
   (간접 의문문: 의문사+주어+동사)
   Do you know where the grocery store is?
   (간접 의문문: 의문사+주어+동사)

2. It's in front of ~: ~앞에 있다
   across the street from ~: ~길 건너 있다
   next to ~: ~옆에 있다
   between A and B: A와 B 사이에 있다
   at the corner of A and B: A와 B의 모퉁이에 있다

3. Is it far? (먼가요?)
   How far is it? (얼마나 멀죠?)

4. You can't miss it. (반드시 찾을 수 있을 거예요)
   I bet you can find it easily.

5. I'm new here.
   I'm a stranger here myself. (저도 여기 초행입니다)

*The world is a book and those who
do not travel read only one page.*

세계는 한 권의 책이다. 여행하지 않는 사람은 단지
그 책의 한 페이지만 읽는 것이다.

- St. Augustine -

Dialogue 1. 관광정보 묻기

Traveler: Excuse me!

Where is the tourist information center?

Lady : Go straight about 100 meters and it'll be on your right.

Traveler: Thanks.

....

Traveler: I'd like some information about a half-day tour.

Would you recommend a good place to see?

Staff : How about the Polynesian Cultural Center?

It's an outdoor theme park where you can experience the

Polynesian culture.

Notes

▶ tourist information center: 관광 안내소

▶ I'd like + 명사

I'd like to + 동사

▶ How about ~ = What about ~: ~ 어떠세요?

▶ half-day tour: 반일 관광

one-day tour: 일일 관광

▶ outdoor theme park: 야외 테마파크

대화 1. 관광정보 묻기

여행자: 실례합니다. 관광 안내소가 어디에 있나요?
숙녀   : 100 미터 정도 쭉 가시면, 오른쪽에 있을 겁니다.
여행자: 감사해요.
          …………

여행자: 반일 관광에 대한 정보를 좀 원합니다.
        구경하기 좋은 곳 추천해 주시겠어요?
직원   : 폴리네시아 문화센터 어떠세요?
        폴리네시아 문화를 체험할 수 있는 야외 테마파크입니다.

Dialogue 2. 입장료 문의

Traveler: How much is the admission fee?

Staff　　: 40 dollars for adults and 20 dollars for children.
　　　　　　It's free for children under 3.

Traveler: Two adults and one child, please.

Staff　　: The total comes to 100 dollars.

Traveler: By the way, when does the show start?

Staff　　: It starts in 20 minutes.

Traveler: How long does the show run?

Staff　　: It runs for about 2 hours.

Notes

▸ How much is the admission fee?
　What's the admission fee? (입장료가 얼마인가요?)

▸ admission fee = entrance fee (입장료)
▸ by the way: 그런데요 (화제 전환 시 사용)
▸ run: ① 달리다 (자동사)
　　　　② 운영하다 (타동사)
　　　　③ (연극, 영화, 공연이) 공연되다, 상연되다 (자동사)
▸ Do you have a student discount? (학생 할인되나요?)
　　　　　　　　a military discount? (군인/군인가족 할인되나요?)
　　　　　　　　a senior discount? (경로우대 되나요?)

* 국제학생증(ISEC)은 수정의 비용을 내고 필수 구비서류를 갖추면 온라인으로 발급신청이 가능합니다. 초등학교 이상 학생인 경우 입장료, 숙박시설, 교통비 할인 등 혜택이 많으므로 준비해 가면 좋습니다.

대화 2. 입장료 문의

여행자: 입장료는 얼마입니까?

직원 : 어른은 40불, 어린이는 20불입니다.
　　　 3살 미만은 무료입니다.

여행자: 어른 둘, 어린이 하나 부탁합니다.

직원 : 총 100불입니다.

여행자: 그런데요, 공연은 언제 시작하나요?

직원 : 20분 후에 시작해요.

여행자: 공연은 얼마 동안 하나요?

직원 : 약 2시간 동안요.

Dialogue 3. 사진 촬영

1. 촬영 금지

Traveler: Can I take a picture?

Lady　　: No, you are not allowed to take a picture or a video here.

Traveler: Oh, I see.

Notes

▶ take a picture: 사진 찍다

　take a video: 비디오 촬영하다

▶ be allowed to ~: ~하도록 허락되다

　be not allowed to ~: ~하도록 허락되지 않다

▶ I see.: 알았어요. (I know가 아님)

1. 촬영 금지

여행자: 사진 찍어도 될까요?

숙녀　: 아니요. 사진이나 비디오 찍으시면 안 됩니다.

여행자: 오, 알았어요.

2. 촬영 부탁

Traveler: Would you take a picture for me?

Lady   : Sure.

Traveler: Would you get that in the background?

Lady   : No problem. Say "Cheese!"

Traveler: Cheese! Can you take one more shot?

Lady   : Okay. I'll take one more.

Traveler: Your costume is so beautiful.

         Can I take a picture with you?

Lady   : Sure. Get closer together.

Notes

▸ Would you take a picture **for** me?

  Would you take a picture **of** me?

  (제 사진 좀 찍어 주시겠어요?) (전치사 for, of 모두 가능)

▸ Would you ~ Could you ~

  Can you ~   Will you ~

  (모두 상대에게 요청할 때 쓸 수 있는 표현.

  Would you, Could you가 Can you, Will you보다 더 공손)

▸ shot: ① 총기 발사, 발포

       ② 사진

       ③ 주사 (한 대)

       ④ (특히 독한 술) 한 잔, 한 모금

       ⑤ 커피 원액

          (Please add one more shot. 샷 하나 더 넣어 주세요)

2. 촬영 부탁

여행자: 제 사진 좀 찍어 주시겠어요?

숙녀　: 네.

여행자: 저것이 배경으로 나오게 해 주시겠어요?

숙녀　: 네. "치즈!" 하세요.

여행자: 치즈! 한 장 더 찍어 주시겠어요?

숙녀　: 네, 한 장 더 찍을게요.

여행자: 의상이 아주 아름다우시네요.
**　　　당신과 한 장 찍어도 될까요?**

숙녀　: 네. 가까이 오세요.

3. 촬영 후

Lady   : You look great in this picture.

             You are very photogenic.

Traveler 1: Thanks. I like it.

Lady   : You look much better in person.

Traveler 2: I look terrible in pictures.

             So I don't like to be photographed.

Notes

▶ You look better <u>in person</u>.

   = You look better <u>in real life</u>. (당신은 실물이 더 나으세요)

You look **much** better in person.

You look **much** better in real life. (실물이 **훨씬** 더 나으세요)

▶ 비교급 강조 부사: far, still, even, much, a lot

You look **much** better in person.

You look **far** better in person.

You look **still** better in person.

You look **even** better in person.

You look **a lot** better in person.

(당신은 실물이 **훨씬** 더 나으세요)

3. 촬영 후

숙녀　　: 당신 사진 잘 나왔네요. 사진 참 잘 받으세요.

여행자 1: 고마워요. 사진 맘에 드네요.

숙녀　　: 당신은 실물이 훨씬 더 나으세요.

여행자 2: 전 사진이 잘 안 나와요.

　　　　　그래서 전 사진 찍는 걸 싫어해요.

More Expressions

1. Can you take a picture **for** me?
   Can you take a picture **of** me?
   (제 사진 좀 찍어 주실래요?)

   → <u>상대에게 내 사진을 찍어 달라고 부탁할 때</u> 사용.

2. Can I take a picture **for** you?
   Can I take a picture **of** you?
   (제가 당신을 좀 찍어도 될까요?)

   → <u>내가 상대방을 찍고 싶을 때</u> 허락을 구하는 표현.

3. Can I take a picture **with** you?
   (제가 당신과 함께 사진 좀 찍어도 될까요?)

   → <u>상대와 함께 찍고 싶을 때</u> 허락을 구하는 표현.

Make voyages. Attempt them.
There's nothing else.

여행을 떠나라. 그것을 시도하라.
그 외에 무엇이 있겠는가.

- Tennessee Williams -

병원

Dialogue 1. 접수대에서

Staff　　: May I help you?

Traveler: My name is Yura Jeong.

　　　　　I've got an appointment.

Staff　　: Ms. Jeong⋯ Ah, yes.

　　　　　The appointment was ten thirty.

　　　　　Now it's twenty to eleven.

Traveler: Sorry I am late.

Staff　　: It's OK. Please wait for a moment.

　　　　　I think we can fit you in.

Traveler: Oh Good. Thank you.

Staff　　: Do you have health insurance?

Traveler: No, I don't. I am a traveler.

Notes

▶ I've got an appointment.
　I have an appointment.

　I've got = I have
　You've got = You have
　She's got = She has
　He's got = He has

▶ It's twenty to eleven. (11시 20분 전이에요)
　= It's ten forty. (10시 40분이에요)

대화 1. 접수대에서

직원　: 도와 드릴까요?

여행자: 제 이름은 정유라예요. 예약한 게 있는데요.

직원　: Ms. 정. 아, 네. 예약이 10시 30분이었네요.
　　　지금 11시 20분 전이에요.

여행자: 늦어서 미안합니다.

직원　: 괜찮아요. 잠시 기다리세요.
　　　해 드릴 수 있을 것 같아요.

여행자: 아, 잘됐네요. 감사합니다.

직원　: 건강 보험 있으세요?

여행자: 아니오. 전 여행자입니다.

※ 시간 말하기

3:00
It's three o'clock.

3:10
It's three ten.
It's ten past three.

3:15
It's three fifteen.
It's quarter past three.

3:30
It's three thirty.
It's half past three.

3:40
It's three forty.
It's twenty to four.

3:45
It's three forty five.
It's quarter to four.

3:55
It's three fifty five.
It's five to four.

시간 말하는 방법

1. 시간, 분 순서대로 말하기
2. 15분, 45분은 quarter, 30분은 half,
   '전'은 'to', '후'는 'past'를 사용하여 말하기

Dialogue 2. 진료

Doctor : Good morning! Please come in.

What are your symptoms?

Traveler: I have a sore throat. And I have trouble swallowing.

Doctor : Would you open your mouth nice and wide?

Traveler: OK.

Doctor : Now I need to put this thermometer in your ear to take your temperature. There we go.

Is that OK?

Traveler: Yes, that's OK.

Doctor : Your tonsils are swollen, and your temperature is a little high. I'm going to prescribe some antibiotics. Drink a lot of warm water, get some rest, and come back in two days.

Notes

▶ What are your symptoms? (증상이 어떠세요?)

What's the problem? (어디가 안 좋으세요?)

What seems to be the problem? (어디가 안 좋으신 것 같아요?)

▶ I have trouble(difficulty) ~ing: ~하는 데 문제(어려움)가 있다

▶ nice and wide: 크게

대화 2. 진료

의사　: 안녕하세요! 들어오세요.
　　　　증상이 어떠세요?
여행자: 목이 아프고요, 삼키는 데 어려움이 있어요.
의사　: 입을 크게 벌려 보시겠어요?
여행자: 네.
의사　: 이 체온계를 귀에 넣고 체온을 잴 거예요.
　　　　자, 시작합니다. 괜찮죠?
여행자: 네, 괜찮아요.
의사　: 편도가 부어있고 체온이 좀 높아요.
　　　　항생제를 처방해 드릴게요.
　　　　따뜻한 물 많이 드시고, 휴식을 취하시고, 이틀 후에 다시 오세요.

More Expressions

1. I've got a cut on my finger. (제 손가락을 베었어요)
2. I've got a blister on my foot. (발에 물집이 생겼어요)
3. I've got scratches on my wrist. (손목에 찰과상을 입었어요)
4. I've got bruises on my leg. (다리에 타박상을 입었어요)
5. I've got a rash on my arm. (팔에 발진이 생겼어요)
   * I've got = I have got = I have

6. I have a headache. (두통)
       a toothache. (치통)
       a cold. (감기)
       a fever. (열)
       a sore throat. (목이 아픔)
       a runny nose. (콧물)
       a stuffy nose. (코 막힘)
       a cough. (기침)
       a stomachache. (위통)
       an upset stomach. (위통)
       a backache. (요통)
       a tightness in my chest. (가슴이 답답)
       a bug bite. (벌레에 물림)
       a hangover. (숙취)
       the flu. (독감)

I have indigestion. (소화불량이에요)

    diarrhea[daiəríə] = I have the runs. (설사해요)

    ringing in my ears. (이명이 있어요)

    jet lag. (시차로 인한 피로감/시차증이 있어요)

    no appetite. (식욕이 없어요)

I have <u>motion</u> sickness. = I am <u>motion</u> sick. (멀미해요)

car	car	(차멀미)
sea	sea	(뱃멀미)
air	air	(비행기 멀미)

My tonsils are swollen. (편도가 부었어요)

I've been sneezing. (재채기를 계속 해요)

I feel dizzy. (현기증이 나요)

I feel nauseous. (구역질을 해요)

I'm constipated. (변비가 있어요)

I twisted my ankle. (발목을 삐었어요)

I broke my arm. (팔이 부러졌어요)

I burned my hand. (손을 데었어요)

I cut my finger. (손가락을 베었어요)

It hurts around here. (이 근처가 아파요)

I ache all over. (온몸이 쑤셔요)

I'm out of it. (기운이 없어요)

I am homesick. (집 생각이 나요)

※ 이명, 시차증, 멀미, 설사, 소화불량 등의 단어 앞엔 관사 'a, an, the'를 사용하지 않습니다.

A man travels over in search of what he need,
and returns home to find it.

인간은 필요한 것을 찾아 세상을 여행하지만

집에 돌아와서 그것을 발견하게 된다.

- George Augustus Moore -

Traveler   : Can you fill this prescription?

Pharmacist: Sure. Take this medicine three times a day after meals.

It should not be taken on an empty stomach.

It can cause stomachache and nausea.

Traveler   : **Thank you for your kind explanation.**

Pharmacist: You're welcome.

Notes

▶ fill prescription: 처방전대로 약을 조제하다

▶ nausea: 메스꺼움, 구역질

▶ empty stomach: 공복

여행자: 이 처방전대로 약을 지어 주실래요?

약사   : 네. 식후 하루 세 번 이 약을 드세요.

공복에는 들지 마세요. 위통과 메스꺼움을 초래할 수 있거든요.

여행자: 친절한 설명에 감사드립니다.

약사   : 별말씀을요.

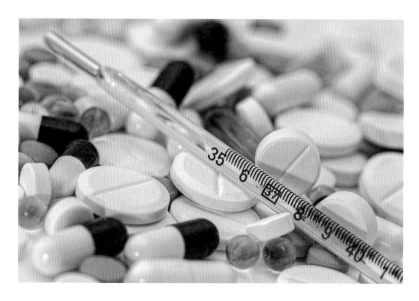

꿈이 있는 **여행 영어**

ⓒ 김계희, 2023

초판 1쇄 발행 2023년 6월 30일
　　2쇄 발행 2023년 9월 11일

지은이　　김계희
펴낸이　　이기봉
편집　　　좋은땅 편집팀
펴낸곳　　도서출판 좋은땅
주소　　　서울특별시 마포구 양화로12길 26 지월드빌딩 (서교동 395-7)
전화　　　02)374-8616~7
팩스　　　02)374-8614
이메일　　gworldbook@naver.com
홈페이지　www.g-world.co.kr

ISBN　979-11-388-2094-3 (03740)